Praise for Deborah Taylor-Hough's Freezer Cooking Methods
. . .

"Frozen Assets will prove to be the hands-down authority on once-a-month cooking."
—Susan R. Sands, Publisher, *Home Words Magazine*

"This book offers relief to those tired of eating restaurant fare or expensive, over packaged convenience foods at the end of a hard day. Recommended..."
—*Library Journal*

"...contains recipe ideas, plus detailed instructions on how to get the maximum value from your food dollar, while also slashing meal preparation times. If you are into efficiency and want a guide to reorganizing your culinary life, this book is a must-have."
—Amazon.com

"Finally, a realistic way to combine the cost effectiveness of cooking from scratch with the convenience of quick and easy meals!"—Mary Hunt, Editor & Publisher, *Cheapskate Monthly Newsletter*

"This cookbook is a necessity for anyone trying to save time and money while still providing a nutritious home-cooked meal."—*Home Cooking Magazine*

"This book belongs in every family's kitchen! One of the best time and money-savers a busy family can have." —Gary Foreman, Editor, *The Dollar Stretcher*

"There are shopping lists and recipes for two-week and 30-day meal plans. There's even a 10-day plan designed to eliminate cooking over the Christmas and New Year holidays. What a stress reliever!"—*The Daily News*, Washington

"Finally a book that is so cooking-friendly ANYONE can follow the steps." —Sherry Stacy, Weekly Radio Host, Recipes for Life on KVSN

"Whether you cook for one month or one week, I am sure everyone can reap benefit from this book."—Keith C. Heirdorn, Publisher, *Living Gently Quarterly*

"Frozen Assets will be at the top of my recommended books list!"— Rebecca Stuck, Advice Columnist, Ask Miss Frugal

"And she's done an impressive job with this book, which outlines step-by-step the shopping, cooking and freezing processes that have worked so well..."—Copley News Service

"...details a plan for cooking and freezing in quantity, with grocery lists, shopping lists, storage tips and dollar-stretching hints. The recipes are simple and straightforward, using everyday ingredients."—*Atlanta Journal*

"A perfect gift for a busy homemaker."—*The News-Herald* Newspapers

"...provides shopping lists and delicious recipes that will help you save time in the kitchen and money in the grocery store."—The Oak Ridger, Tennessee

"Taylor-Hough's recipes are easy, with a minimum amount of ingredients and labor. And she presents the plan with an eye toward flexibility, allowing cooks to adapt the freeze-ahead plan to their own palates and checkbooks."—*Johnson City Press*

"...offers kid-tested recipes that are easy and affordable."—*The Oregonian*

"...cooks looking to save time without resorting to expensive convenience food will find this book helpful." —*Herald-Journal*

"...[this] book outlines a step-by-step plan to one dedicated day in the kitchen that will provide breakfasts, lunches and dinners for the following month."—*Detroit News*

"...a cookbook well worth a second look."—*The Pilot*, North Carolina

"...just about everyone will find the planning and organizational tips valuable..."
—The Light Connection

"...the book is a one-stop resource for those looking to increase their time at the family table and decrease time spent in the kitchen and drive-through lanes." —*The Cookbook Collectors' Exchange*

Cook for a Day, Eat for a Month

Frozen Assets Lite & Easy

Cook for a Day, Eat for a Month

Frozen Assets Lite & Easy

Deborah Taylor-Hough

CHAMPION PRESS LTD.

CHAMPION PRESS, LTD. • MILWAUKEE, WISCONSIN

CHAMPION PRESS, LTD.
MILWAUKEE, WISCONSIN

LCCN 98-072249

Cataloging in Publication Data
Taylor-Hough, Deborah
    Frozen assets: how to cook for a day and eat for a month / Deborah Taylor-Hough.
    p.cm.
    Includes index.
    ISBN 1-891400-28-2

    1. Make-ahead cookery 2. Frozen foods. 3. Quantity cooking. I. Title

    TX610.T39. 2002
        641.5'55.

For more information contact: Champion Press, Ltd., 8689 N. Port Washington Rd. #329, Milwaukee, WI 53217, www.championpress.com

ISBN 1-891400-28-2
Manufactured in the United States of America   30 29 28 27 26 25 24 23 22 21
Book Cover Design by David Quintero, Quintero Design.
Book Text Design by Kathy Campbell, Wildwood Studio.

Dedication

This book is dedicated to my mother-in-law,
Jean Hough, whose kitchen organizational skills,
fabulous parties and gifts of hospitality are truly
awe-inspiring. Thank you for your example!

Acknowledgments

I just want to thank everyone who offered moral support or had input into this book during its production and writing: Brook Noel, Leanne Ely, Q, Catherine Levison, Lisa Morales, Miriam Roush, Karen Jogerst, Teri Brown, Larry Wilson, Gary Foreman, Gina Dalquest, Chris Saunders, *Simple Times* readers, participants from my frugal living message board, the Frozen-Assets email list members, Stuart, Kelsey, Ian, Shannon, Dad.

Contents

CHAPTER ONE

Frozen Assets

Those of you familiar with my first book may be wondering, "Why another *Frozen Assets* book?"

Good question. The original *Frozen Assets: how to cook for a day and eat for a month* was written specifically to help readers learn realistic and inexpensive ways to apply bulk cooking methods to their regular family meal planning. The emphasis in the first *Frozen Assets* was on two commodities in high demand: time and money. For many, making the switch to eating home cooked meals every night rather than a regular diet of fast food and pizza delivery also created a healthier lifestyle. However, over the years, readers have contacted me looking for simple meal plans with lower-fat recipes. I've also heard from readers looking for vegetarian fare to add to their freezer-meal recipe collections.

The recipes in *Frozen Assets Lite and Easy* are an answer for those of you looking to apply the same timesaving and easy cooking methods to lower-calorie meals. While you can still expect to cut your budget significantly by using these bulk preparation methods, the lower-fat recipes tend to use more expensive ingredients than the original recipes of the first *Frozen Assets* book. Using the recipes and meal plans in that book I was able to shave $400 off our family food budget during a time when saving money was a top priority in my life. This actually added up to $24,000 over a five-year period!

Yet the principles of *Frozen Assets Lite & Easy* cooking will still allow you to trim your food budget as well as your fat. Buying in bulk and using all the foods before they perish will greatly reduce trips to the store; the chance of impulse purchasing and throwing away yet another vegetable gone bad. It will also allow you to take advantage of store sales and specials as you'll see when we explore the mini-session methods.

Healthy Transitions

The reasons people choose to start eating healthier are varied. Some of us want (or need) to shed a few extra pounds. Some are interested in a generally healthier lifestyle. Some have more philosophical reasons for avoiding meat or other food items. Others face health-related dietary restrictions.

In the food department of life, I've definitely been my own worst enemy over the years. Eating healthy has long been appealing to me . . . but not so easily attainable. I can still remember the first time I browsed through my well-loved copy of *Laurel's Kitchen* and dreamed of all the whole foods my family would soon be eating. And eat healthy, we did! For awhile...

I remember baking my own breads, tenderly kneading each loaf by hand in my favorite over-sized mixing bowl (this was in the good old days before automatic bread machines). I relished the entire process of baking fresh homemade bread—the taste, the feel, the smell. For awhile...

I remember happily replacing meat in our regular family recipes with tofu and texturized vegetable protein (TVP). What a great feeling to feed my family lower-fat, healthier foods. With a tremendous sense of accomplishment, I prepared our new healthier meals. For awhile . . .

Are you beginning to sense a pattern here? It seemed my best intentions were constantly being way-laid by life. Whether it was a financial setback, a premature baby, an extended time of bed-rest during a difficult pregnancy, or an overly busy schedule, something always pushed me back into the realm of what was normal and comfortable in the food department of my life. The old expression, "Life's what happens when you make other plans," was certainly holding true in my eating and cooking regimens. I continually found myself coasting back down to lower levels of eating. I was on a never-ending roller coaster ride. And I wanted off.

I knew I'd hit rock bottom when I was starting to plan our family meals around the local fast food restaurant's choice of children's meal toys. Have you ever known anyone on a first name basis with the pizza delivery guy, the kids calling out when the doorbell rang, "Mommy, Bob's here with the pizza!"? The regular lady at the local drive-thru would comment about how she hadn't seen us for awhile if we didn't come to her window for a week or so.

Things were bad. Really bad.

But I knew I needed more than just an outward change in my eating habits. I needed to find some sort of inner motivation that would keep me on the right path no matter what distractions and detours life sent my way.

The biggest obstacle that kept me from pursuing healthy eating habits was my personal time constraints. Like many people today, I didn't have time to get home-cooked meals on the table regularly—much less take the time to actually prepare something nutritious and healthy.

Then something happened that completely changed my wishy-washy approach to healthful eating.

One morning I was showering and discovered what every woman dreads: a lump. A sizeable lump. Suddenly I was at the doctor's office having x-rays and ultrasounds, and before I really had time to fathom the full repercussions of this

new chapter in my life, I was being scheduled for a surgical lumpectomy and biopsy. The earliest they could schedule the procedure was several weeks away, so I found myself in "waiting mode," trying not to obsess about my health, but finding myself helplessly evaluating everything in my life.

It seemed that in one swift, life-changing moment I'd gone from peacefully going about my quiet little life to suddenly examining every moment and activity in light of the question, "What if... ?" What if I have cancer? What if I get horribly sick? What if I die? What if I don't live to see my children grow up? What if this is my last summer here on Earth? What if...

My entire life was now under a high-power microscope. I'd find myself looking at an activity and thinking, "Is this how I would want to spend my time if this were the last week of my life?" More often than not, the answer was a resounding, "No!" Suddenly everything stood out like a relief map. It was easy to identify priorities in a way I never had before. I had lived for a long time with a clear set of priorities before me, but my priorities took on new meaning as I sensed a new urgency.

My children. My husband. My faith. My church. These priorities suddenly grew in importance as my focus changed. Other activities like writing, public speaking, Internet activities and even mundane things like housework lessened their hold over my life. Not that those things ceased to be important but their placement in the way I chose to spend my time and energy changed.

I even found myself looking at where I lived and deciding that if I was facing the end of my time, one of my biggest regrets was living at the end of a cul-de-sac in a standard housing development. My heart had always been in the country with horses and acreage. If my life was over, I found that I truly regretted not having done what was necessary to make that dream come true somehow. Raising my children in suburbia wasn't what I'd wanted for my life. I found myself wondering when I'd started living someone else's dreams.

But probably the biggest refocusing that occurred was in the area of my physical health. For many years I'd been eating a poor diet and living a sedentary lifestyle. And my poor body showed it. Out of shape, overweight, out of breath.

Suddenly I confronted my physical health in a new way and decided I needed to make some changes . . . now! In addition to regular aerobic exercise and strength training, I also decided to change my eating habits. Nothing drastic. I didn't set out to lose forty pounds in two weeks or anything similar. But by eating lower-fat, healthier meals and being careful about not overdoing it on sweets or second helpings, I hoped to change my health in simple—yet profound—ways. After starting this lower-fat, more balanced approach to eating, I lost ten pounds in the first week . . . and I wasn't doing anything drastic at all. My goal hadn't necessarily been weight loss. I'm much more concerned with maintaining a healthier lifestyle in general. But as my body reacts to the new ways of eating and exercising, I'm sure the weight will come off too. But in the meantime, I'm feeling better and stronger than I have in a long, long time.

This book contains many of the recipes I've been preparing for myself and my family lately. Hopefully the meal plans will help you and your family in your pursuit of healthy, vital lives.

CHAPTER TWO

Saving Time,
Saving Money

Well, this deal is for real. I have a commodity
to offer that's more valuable than gold . . . or land . . . or diamonds. That
precious gem I can offer you is called: Time!

Wouldn't you love to free up quantities of time each and every day? Time
that could be spent sitting down with your spouse on the couch, actually
putting your feet up after work for a few undisturbed moments? Wouldn't your
children relish curling up in a parent's lap for a cuddle and a chapter from the
family's latest read-aloud book before dinner?

And wouldn't you really love having an easy answer to that perennial
question, "What's for dinner?"

What's for dinner tonight could be as simple as something you whip
together in fifteen to twenty minutes: Salisbury Steak, homemade fish chowder,
Aunt Emily's favorite lasagna, roast turkey with all the fixings, marinated
chicken breasts or whatever else your family enjoys eating. And you won't spend
an hour or two slaving over a hot stove every night to achieve this culinary
miracle. It might just require the minor effort of throwing a baking dish into the
oven and forgetting it for an hour. Or stirring something over a stovetop burner
just until it's heated through. Make a salad, slice some French bread fresh from
the corner bakery and voila', you have a dinner that would make Martha proud!

Crisis Meal Planning

If your home is anything like mine, you've probably found that five o'clock each
evening is one of the most hectic times of the day. Mom and dad are just
finishing up a long day of work at home or at the office. The kids are hungry
and tired after a full day of school and afternoon sports. It's time to fix supper or
at least we should be getting dinner started if we want to eat a meal before
midnight! But what's for dinner tonight? Well, your guess is probably as good as
mine . . . and it seems like more often than not, nobody knows! So the whole

family hops in the car and heads through the local drive-thru for the third time this week.

Someone I know once called it "crisis" meal planning. Each night's dinner is the latest in a string of mealtime crisis management decisions. Everyone's tired. The kids are hungry. The whining is starting in earnest. What's a parent to do?

"What will we have to eat? Um . . . well . . . I just heard that Fred's Diner is having a sale on cheeseburgers this week. Let's go! Everyone in the car!"

Rather than planning ahead to prevent panic and poor nutritional choices, many families coast through their day without giving a thought to dinner and then discover they've crashed headlong into that nightly mealtime crisis once again.

Cooking ahead for the freezer can be the answer to this all-too-frequent mealtime dilemma. The process of cooking an entire month's worth meals in one day is an efficient and cost-saving alternative for many families, but spending eight hours in the kitchen is daunting for some who would like to try this method. The mini-session is the perfect answer for these people.

Whether you choose to triple recipes during your regular meal preparations or cook a full month of meals at a time or simply choose a mini-session or two, you'll find this method will save not only your time, but also your money and sanity. No more crisis meal planning; you'll have dinner on the table regularly with little more fuss than heating a thawed freezer meal and adding a quick salad or side dish.

The Art of the Mini-Session

I've discovered as people become more adept and experienced at cooking for the freezer, they often switch from doing a full one-day-each-month cooking frenzy to using a simpler process referred to as "mini-sessions" in this book. A mini-session consists of choosing one main ingredient, such as chicken, and then preparing a group of chicken recipes in a single afternoon or evening. A mini-session usually involves only an hour or two of cooking rather than the eight to ten hours often required for a complete month of cooking.

By waiting for main ingredients to go on sale at your local market, you can stock up on large quantities and take advantage of great prices. For example, if you stock up on lean ground beef at this week's sale, a relatively short mini-session could easily supply you with five to ten ground beef meals tucked away in the freezer. When chicken goes on sale later in the month, you can add another five to ten meals to your personal stash of *Frozen Assets*. Simply by purchasing and cooking in bulk as you follow the sale flyers from the grocery store, you can save a great deal of time and money without ever investing an entire day in a monthly cooking session.

This new book, *Frozen Assets Lite and Easy*, focuses on the mini-session method, but that doesn't mean it won't be flexible and easily adapted for those readers who prefer the one-day-a-month procedure. If you want to do a full month of cooking in one day, simply double or triple several mini-sessions and then prepare these sessions together in one day. A full day of cooking for the freezer is essentially just a series of mini-sessions. Most cooks will prepare all their ground meat recipes together, then the chicken recipes, then spaghetti sauce based recipes, then vegetarian or bean recipes.

The great thing about breaking this all down into mini-sessions is that it allows you to build a month's worth of recipes around your family's specific tastes. Instead of trying to pull apart a 30-Day Meal Plan and change one disliked recipe, you can build your menus around mini-sessions that the family enjoys. Many people also find it easier to build their own mini-sessions to incorporate into their *Frozen Assets* regimen. Be flexible. Take your favorite recipes from *Frozen Assets One* and build them into a mini-session. Build your own mini-sessions. Use the mini-sessions offered in this book. Combine all three ideas. Whatever you choose—a boundless array of easy-meal choices await you!

But Isn't it a Leftover?

Many people worry that eating meals from the freezer will be like having leftovers every night. But it's not. You won't be eating something that's been cooked completely, and then reheated, and then reheated again. You're eating food that's either been frozen before cooking so it's cooked up fresh on serving day, or you're eating food that's been cooked just until barely done, frozen and then reheated just enough  to serve. If food is cooked and stored properly, frozen dinners can be as tasty as fresh.

CHAPTER THREE

Easier Cooking
for Easier Living

I first started cooking ahead for the time saving benefits. It helped bring our family together again around the table. But I was quickly surprised by another benefit that I didn't foresee. Our grocery bill went down by almost $400 per month! I couldn't believe it! Some of the money we saved was due to the fact that we had been eating out quite frequently, quickly running down to the corner for 59 cent tacos because I didn't have time to cook dinner. Now we always have time for dinner at home—we eat out when we want to, not because we feel we have to. Going out to eat has become a special treat rather than an expensive and unhealthy way of life.

By cooking ahead, I was able to begin buying commonly used items in bulk. I was also planning my menus ahead of time. Just the planning ahead and bulk buying saves a lot of money. But $400 per month? Wow! And that was the average I was shaving off our grocery bill each month. Sometimes we saved even more than that. This method also eliminates waste, and because I don't go to the store nearly as often as I used to, it also cuts down on those expensive impulse buys at the market.

I can take full advantage of sales at the grocery store, planning menus around the weekly specials. If ground beef is on sale, I'll buy a large amount and then prepare a quantity of ground beef recipes and put them in the freezer. Rather than doing a full month of cooking, I'll do what I refer to as a Ground Beef Mini-Session. This involves preparing a week or two of ground beef recipes to intersperse with the chicken or tofu recipes I prepared during an earlier chicken or tofu mini-session. With a combination of these mini-sessions I can stash away *Frozen Assets* for the next two or three months. But in addition to the time and money saving benefits, I discovered many other perks.

Hospitality

Frozen meals can be used for hospitality and outreach. Dinner parties are a breeze. If we want to spontaneously invite people over after church, it's not a difficult ordeal. I know I have things in the freezer that I can quickly and easily heat and serve. You can have meals available for the sick or for people in need. Bringing a couple of frozen meals to a new mother or a grieving family can bring a touch of sanity to an otherwise stressful time of life. I don't even have to think about it or plan for it. I just grab something from the freezer and go.

Financial Freedom

Not only did cooking ahead solve the meal planning and time issues, it also provided me with a way to help our family's financial situation. Money was quite tight and I had been thinking of getting a part-time job to help make ends meet. I found cutting back a bit on what I was spending on groceries could mean the difference between remaining at home with my children or going back to work. I wouldn't cut back on the amount of food we ate, so we still ate well, but by being conscientious about meal planning and buying on sale, we shaved sizeable amounts off our monthly food budget. Saving $400 per month from our approximately $700 per month grocery budget became "my part time job". Over the course of five years, I spent $24,000 less on groceries!

No More Kitchen Slavery

During those rare times when I run out of my *Frozen Assets* stash, it's a rude awakening to see just how "daily" food preparation is in a busy home. As I often say when doing my workshops—I like cooking—I just don't like it every day! Between all the planning and actual preparation for each meal, it can begin to seem like the kitchen is a harsh taskmaster, not even allowing time off for good behavior. The daily-ness of cooking wears us down quickly. By having meals ready to go in the freezer, I find that the joy of cooking has been restored for me. When I do decide to cook a special meal, it's a joy again and not just another chore to be accomplished as quickly as possible. I also have more time and energy for fun cooking—baking cookies with my children or making fresh, hot gingerbread on a cold winter evening.

Restoring the Family Dinner Hour

Recently, there was a story in my local newspaper about the disappearance of the family dinner hour. With more and more double-income families and children involved in numerous after school and sports activities, the family dinner hour has gone the way of the dinosaur.

Yet my family sits down together for dinner at least five times each week. How often do you sit down as a family at the table for a leisurely meal? Four times a week? Twice? Once? I'm not super woman; I'm simply someone who discovered a way to reap the benefits of advanced planning and preparation. Now these benefits can be yours. I'll show you how to make it happen step-by-step. If you'd like to restore this time-honored tradition in your home, cooking for the freezer can be the solution. So what are you waiting for? Let's get started.

CHAPTER FOUR

Cooking for the Freezer 101

I recommend that people start this process gradually. If the idea of a full month of cooking sounds overwhelming, start small. If two weeks sounds more do-able, try cooking ahead for two weeks. Or one week.

But if cooking for even a week at a time sounds like more than you can fathom, try this: In the course of your normal cooking, triple your recipes. If you're preparing lasagna, make three—one for eating tonight and two for the freezer. Tomorrow night do the same thing with a different recipe. After one week of tripling your regular meals and freezing two, you'll have two weeks of meals with almost no extra effort. It's really not much harder to prepare three lasagnas than it is to prepare one. Or make a large pot of spaghetti sauce rather than a single family serving and freeze the extras in meal-size servings.

If you think cooking ahead is a process you'd like to try, but you're unsure of the amount of work involved, ease into it. Start out doubling and tripling recipes as you go through your week. Maybe do a ground beef mini-session next time there's a sale at the grocery store. What you will find is that you will start saving time, you'll start saving money, and you won't be doing this in an overwhelming or difficult manner. Each time you pull one of those meals out of the freezer, you'll be pleased.

Small Freezer Syndrome

Many people tell me they only have a small fridge-top freezer so they don't think they can do a full month of meals. That was my excuse for not trying this method at first but I've found with practice, I can pack a full thirty meals in my refrigerator freezer. The last time I did a big cooking day, I counted forty-four meals in my small freezer. I have a separate freezer now, but I usually use it for stocking things like ice cream or bread I find on sale at the bakery thrift store. I keep my prepared meals in the small kitchen freezer where they're easily accessible.

Probably the most practical suggestion for people with a small freezer is to use zip-top freezer bags. The bags take up a lot less room than bulkier storage containers such as plastic boxes or aluminum pans. If you take your freezer bags and freeze them flat, then you can stand them on end after they're frozen solid. Your freezer shelf will look like it contains LP record albums filled with frozen food and you won't experience a landslide of frozen packages when you open the freezer door.

Clear out all non-essentials on cooking day if you only have a small freezer. When I only had the small refrigerator-freezer, I would wait until mid-month to stock up on things like ice cream or frozen bread. I used this cooking technique for over three years with only a small fridge-top freezer, so it can be done. It just takes careful planning and packing.

To save space, you can also prepare sauces to serve over pasta or rice, but don't make the pasta or rice ahead of time. Cook the pasta or rice at serving time. Usually the sauce is the time-consuming part of fixing dinner, so by fixing the pasta or rice fresh, it not only tastes better but allows you to use your freezer space more efficiently.

Freezer Containers

I want to assure you that you don't need to hold a party and buy expensive plastic boxes. Any food grade plastic will work. The inexpensive plastic boxes at the grocery store function just fine, but make sure you have storage items with tight fitting, air-tight lids. If you want to invest money in the higher quality plastic boxes, by all means feel free. You definitely get what you pay for, and the fancy expensive home party boxes usually last for many years and come with replacement guarantees. I just want to assure people that you don't *have* to stock your freezer shelves with designer containers. The only plastic freezer containers I own are the inexpensive ones from the grocery store and they have served me well for many years.

You can freeze food items in clean, plastic margarine containers if that's all you have, but the seal isn't really air-tight so don't freeze these items for longer than two weeks or the quality of the food will suffer. It's important to remember that margarine containers are safe to freeze food in (they are made of food grade plastic), but don't reheat your meal in them. They're not microwave-able, and they can seep harmful chemicals into your family's food. Be sure that a plastic container is labeled "microwave safe" before using it to reheat food.

If you have a choice between round and rectangular freezer containers, choose rectangular. These use space more efficiently and take up less room in the freezer.

You can also use disposable aluminum foil pans purchased at the grocery store. These can often be reused several times before needing to be recycled or disposed. Disposable pans are ideal if you're making meals to use to give to others; the recipient doesn't need to worry about returning your pan or casserole dish. If clean up is a huge time-consumer these pans can be easily thrown away to make cleanup painless.

I've built up a good supply of freezer containers by stocking up on bakeware and other freeze-able containers at garage sales and thrift stores. Glass bakeware works fine. When wrapping pans for the freezer, be sure to use good quality heavy-duty freezer foil.

I personally use zip-top freezer bags for most of my food storage needs. Not only do they take up less space than boxes, the bags are inexpensive and easy to use. It's important to buy top quality freezer bags—this isn't the place to cut back, money-wise. There's nothing worse for a freezer-meal cook than to have your entire batch of frozen meals ruined by poor wrapping or freezer bags breaking. I recommend double bagging anything that has a soupy consistency so you don't end up with a watery mess at the bottom of your refrigerator after the meal thaws. Sometimes bags can develop small holes or the zip-top can open slightly.

You can also make your own freezer pans by lining a casserole dish with foil. Put the food in on top of the foil, freeze the meal until it's solid, and then remove the foil and food from the pan. Finish wrapping the meal and put it back in the freezer. When it's time to serve the meal, simply place the foil wrapped meal back into the original pan that was used to mold the frozen meal. Thaw and reheat in the original pan. This method keeps your pans available for other uses during the month.

Labeling Your Freezer Meals

You want to make sure you label everything carefully and accurately. When food is frozen, many meals look the same. One tomato-based meal will look like a dozen other tomato-based meals. You don't want to play "Guess the Freezer Meal" when you're trying to get your family's dinner on the table each night.

I recommend using Sharpie™ brand permanent markers for labeling. You can actually write directly on the freezer bags and even on the aluminum foil wrappings. I want to emphasize: Don't use any other brand of permanent marker to write on your freezer bags or foil. There are other brands of permanent markers, but Sharpie™ is the only one I've found that won't wipe off. I previously worked in a medical lab and we were required to carry a

Sharpie™ with us at all times. The lab managers wouldn't let us use any other brand of marker. We wrote on beakers, test tubes, Petri-dishes and slides, and

then those items went through assorted chemical baths. The labels written with Sharpies™ wouldn't come off. You don't want to lose your labels so it's important to use the best labeler available.

Another way of labeling items stored in freezer bags is to double bag the food and slip a 3"x5" file card with the labeling instructions between the freezer bags. The outer bag and the label can both be reused indefinitely with this method. This can be handy if you prepare the same meals often when you cook for the freezer. You can prepare half a dozen labels ahead of time and not have to spend that time and effort with each cooking experience. Also, make sure to include your reheating instructions on each label. This way you can prep the meal quickly and easily without having to dig through a recipe box or cookbook.

What to Freeze, What Not to Freeze

When I started cooking for the freezer, I was amazed to find more things freeze well then don't. I thought there must be some special criteria for deciphering whether or not a meal would freeze. But almost anything can be frozen. Take a walk down your grocery store's frozen food aisle sometime and just notice the wide variety of items that can be frozen ahead.

Foods that freeze well:

Baked goods (most)
Beans (dry), cooked
Burgers
Breakfast burritos
Breakfast casseroles
Brownies
Cakes
Calzones
Casseroles
Cookies
Egg rolls
Enchiladas
French toast
Fruit sauces
Fudge

Grains, cooked (rice, barley,
  bulgur, couscous)
Hamburger patties, uncooked
Quiche
Quick breads
Lasagna
Main dishes
Manicotti
Marinated meats
Mashed potatoes
Meatballs
Meatloaf
Meat pies
Muffins
Pancakes

Pies	Soups
Pot pies	Stuffed shells
Poultry	Taco/burrito fillings
Roast meats (beef, chicken, lamb, pork)	Tofu
	Turkey
Sandwiches	TVP (texturized vegetable protein)
Sauces	Waffles
Sloppy Joes	

Things that don't freeze well tend to be egg-based sauces, milk or cream based sauces (they separate but can be recombined after thawing), instant rice, raw salad ingredients, stuffed poultry, dishes with dried toppings, baked fruit pies, mayonnaise (unless it's mixed in and used as part of sauce), cottage cheese, raw clams, hard cooked eggs and fried foods.

Cooking for Your Specific Diet

One of the most frequently asked questions I hear about this method of cooking is, "What about vegetarians? How can vegetarians apply this to how they eat?" Freezer cooking for vegetarian eating really isn't a problem. If you're making a meal, take a single serving out, freeze it, reheat it and see how it turns out. If it turns out well, then you have a successful freezer meal to add to your *Frozen Assets* repertoire. I recommend this single-serving trial process for any meal you're not sure will freeze well. Tofu, TVP (texturized vegetable protein) and cooked dry beans all freeze well. Many people say they actually prefer the texture of pre-frozen tofu, it dries out a bit and becomes a little firmer. Also many of the recipes in this book can be prepared without meat, just leave out the meat from the recipe or switch the meat item with your favorite meat substitute.

All of us eat differently. Each family has different things we prefer to eat. I don't necessarily recommend using either of my *Frozen Assets* books as your freezer meal Bible. Don't feel you can only use the recipes in these books and never venture off and use your own recipes. Try several of the meal plans in the books to get started and get a feel for how the process works, but ultimately I hope readers will take these methods and apply them to their own recipes and ways of eating.

Trial and Error

At times this style of cooking can be a bit of a trial and error process. We all make occasional mistakes but we learn from them and move on. I'll share with you some of the things I recommend watching for during meal preparation and planning. Feel free to learn from my experience.

Be sure to keep track of which meals you've used and which ones are still in the freezer. A few times I've forgotten to keep an accurate record and at the end

of the month, found myself staring at four or five bags of spaghetti sauce with nothing else in the freezer for the last week of the month. My family and I didn't want to eat a full week of spaghetti sauce but that was all that was left. If you don't keep track, you may end up with a large amount of one type of meal; ground beef, tofu or lasagna. By planning ahead and keeping track of the meals as you use them, you can space the meals for more of an assortment week by week. I recommend using a magnetic dry-erase board that can hang on the side of your refrigerator. Simply write down what you have put in your freezer and then cross it off once used. This makes it easy to get a quick grasp on what you have and what you need as you do your menu planning.

I've also had noodles completely disappear from my frozen soups. If you cook noodles all the way until they're soft before freezing, when you take your soup out of the freezer, thaw it and reheat it, you'll find you don't have any noodles left. If you want noodles in your soup, wait until you're reheating the soup after freezing and throw the noodles in then. The noodles will cook while the soup is reheating. Or toss the raw noodles into the freezer bag with the soup just before placing the bag in the freezer.

Another tip to remember is: Moderation in all things. I tend to stock up on meats and food items when they go on sale. One time a friend called to let me know a local store was having a sale on ground turkey for forty pounds for $12. I ran down to the store and bought forty pounds of ground turkey. I was so proud of myself! $12? That's at least forty meals worth of meat for a mere pittance. But six months later we still had ground turkey in the freezer that we were working our way through. My family likes ground turkey, but I discovered they didn't like forty pounds worth. If I had purchased ten pounds, I still would've made a wonderful bargain and my family would've been much happier.

I have also created a message board for those *Frozen Asset* Cooks who want to share their tips, recipes and learn more. For further information, go to: http://hometown.aol.com/oamcloop/index.html

CHAPTER FIVE

Creating a 30-Day Meal Plan

Remember, you don't have to do a full month of meals at once. You can choose to do mini-sessions and stock up gradually, or you can do a week or two at a time, but if you want to do a full month of cooking for the freezer, here are the steps.

STEP ONE

Choose ten to fifteen recipes

First, choose ten to fifteen different recipes, depending upon how often your family is willing to eat the same thing over the course of a month. Usually I can get away with feeding my family the same thing three times during a month, so for my family's tastes and preferences, I could prepare ten different recipes, tripling each one for a month's worth of thirty meals. If your family only wants to eat things twice a month, then you would need to choose fifteen different recipes for your month of meals. If your family only wants to eat things once a month, you have a lot more work because you won't be doubling or tripling the recipes. Thirty completely different recipes can be done, it's just a good deal harder and more time-consuming. The fewer individual recipes you use, the better, as far as time, energy and monetary expenditures for this type of cooking.

STEP TWO

Plan your meals for the month

I try to make sure I spread the recipes apart during the month. My family might not be willing to eat the same meal three days in a row, but they're more than happy to eat the same meal if it's spread a week and an half apart. What I do to ensure I've spaced meals properly is take a blank calendar page and fill it out ahead of time. First, I'll figure out what we're going to eat. I'll try to vary things; we want to have a certain number of chicken recipes or ground beef or vegetarian, and I try to divide it up over the course of the month so I can see where I'm going with the monthly meal plan. Otherwise, I might find that I've forgotten to make a variety of meals for the month, maybe forgetting to make chicken recipes, or making a full month of ground beef meals.

Planning ahead really helps when you're making out your monthly menus. You can plan your recipes around what's on sale at the grocery store the week you'll be cooking. I also look through my freezer, refrigerator and cupboards to see what I have on hand to use in the current meal plan.

STEP THREE

Make your shopping list

After you decide what you're going to make, go through your recipes, writing down every single ingredient and the exact amounts that you'll need. Go through your cupboards, refrigerator and freezer, checking off all ingredients you already have on hand, making certain you have the full amount needed. If you need four 16-ounce cans of tomato sauce, you need to make sure that you actually have that total amount in ounces. If you only have two 8-ounce cans of sauce, you'll need to make a note about how many ounces of tomato sauce you still need to purchase.

After you've gone through all your supplies and cupboards, the items still remaining on your list of ingredients will be your shopping list.

STEP FOUR

Gather freezer containers

You'll need to figure out what type of freezer containers you'll be needing and how many. You'll add these items to your shopping list, as well. Take into account aluminum foil, disposable pans, plastic containers, plastic wrap, freezer bags (assorted sizes), labels, marking pens, etc.

STEP FIVE

Prepare your refrigerator & freezer

The most important thing to do before you head to the grocery store is to thoroughly clean out your refrigerator and freezer. You'll need to make room for all the food that you'll be bringing home from the market. It won't be in the refrigerator very long because you'll be adding it into prepared meals to store in the freezer, but you don't want to find yourself staring at a full refrigerator while you're trying to unload multiple bags of groceries full of perishable food items.

If possible, you'll also want to turn the thermostat setting on your freezer to -10 degrees 24 hours before adding large amounts of unfrozen food to your freezer on your cooking day.

STEP SIX

Put away perishables first

After you're done shopping, put away all of your perishables but leave out on the counter your canned goods and anything that doesn't need to be refrigerated overnight. Putting canned goods away just to take them out again in the morning is definitely an inefficient way to use your time and energy at this point. Trust me, any steps saved on that big cooking day will be appreciated.

STEP SEVEN

Separate your recipes

Separate your recipes according to main ingredients or main protein: chicken, ground beef, ham, dried beans, etc. Plan on preparing your recipes in groups according to the main ingredients. Essentially what you're doing on a big cooking day is a series of mini-sessions. For example do all the chicken recipes at one time, then all the ground beef recipes, then all your dry bean recipes.

STEP EIGHT

Prepare ahead

Assemble all necessary utensils ahead of time: pots, pans, measuring cups, measuring spoons, stirring spoons, wire whisks, appliances, bakeware, freezer containers, etc. It's a good idea to have two complete sets of measuring spoons and measuring cups—one for dry ingredients, the other for wet.

Look through your recipes and break them down into individual steps. You'll want to do similar steps together: brown all the ground beef at once, chop all the vegetables, prepare and debone all the chicken, cook all the beans. You don't want to have four or five little sessions of browning ground beef as you go through your recipes; do it all together at one time. I find doing many of those things the night before the big cooking day is very helpful. In an hour and an half the night before, I can quickly prepare spaghetti sauce, brown the ground beef, cook the chicken, chop the onions and celery and grate any cheeses. It saves a great deal of time and effort for the next day.

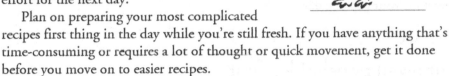

Plan on preparing your most complicated recipes first thing in the day while you're still fresh. If you have anything that's time-consuming or requires a lot of thought or quick movement, get it done before you move on to easier recipes.

STEP NINE

Take care of yourself

Cooking for a month can be a tiring proposition. It's a long day and it's a lot of work, but it doesn't have to be unbearable if you take simple steps to care for yourself.

Remember to think about your comfort and energy level as you go through the day. Get a good night's sleep the night before. Dress comfortably. Wear supportive shoes. This isn't the day to cook barefoot. If you have nurse's shoes, or you've ever worked as a waitress and still have the shoes, that type of footwear is ideal for a long day standing on your feet cooking. Some people even wear hiking boots on cooking day. Wear the most supportive shoes you have in the house. Tie back long hair or wear a hairnet. Put on an apron, even if you don't usually wear one. If you're ever going to make a big mess in the kitchen, this will be the day.

Make it fun: play upbeat music, sing, dance and remember to smile.

Be sure to eat breakfast in the morning. Remember to stop for lunch (and actually sit down while you eat it!). I find I

can get so involved with the cooking process, I forget to eat
all day. Take frequent mini-breaks. Pull up a high stool next to the counter so
you can sit down often. Do as much meal preparation as possible sitting at the
kitchen table.

STEP TEN

Keep it clean

Fill a sink with hot, soapy water so you can wash your pots and pans and
measuring utensils as you go. Wash your hands frequently, especially after
handling raw meats. Tuck a kitchen towel into the waistband of your apron so
it's handy for quickly mopping up messes and spills.

STEP ELEVEN

Prevent overcooking

To prevent overcooking, or that warmed-over taste, slightly undercook foods to
be reheated after freezing. For example, if you're preparing a lasagna requiring a
one hour baking time, cut the time down to 50 minutes, freeze the lasagna at
that point, and then the meal will complete the last ten minutes of cooking
during the reheating process. If you cook things all the way and then freeze and
reheat, you'll get into the realm of feeling you're eating leftovers. Overcooked
food will start tasting "warmed" rather than fresh.

STEP TWELVE

Package, label & freeze your food

Pack food in quantities to be used for family-sized meals. You may also want to
consider packing single-serving sizes for quick lunches. I have a friend whose
husband travels three to five days a week. She prepares individual lasagnas so she
can enjoy home cooked meals when she is alone.

Cool food quickly before placing it in the freezer. Sometimes the quality of
the food will suffer if the food isn't room temperature or cooler when the
freezing process begins. The longer it takes for a food item to freeze completely,
the bigger the ice crystals will be in the finished product. You can cool food by
putting it into the refrigerator for awhile, or fill the bottom of your sink with ice
water and set the pans in the water until the food has cooled (stir the food to
cool it more quickly). Some people who live in areas where it snows and gets

below freezing during the winter will actually cool their food by placing it outside in a snow bank.

You don't want to put hot food directly into plastic freezer bags.

Pack your freezer containers tightly without air pockets, but remember to leave head space of at least one-inch allowing for the expansion of liquid-based meals.

Set meal packages directly onto freezer shelves allowing room for air circulation. After the meals are frozen solid, stack them tightly.

Remove air from your freezer bags by either pressing the air out with your hands, starting at the bottom and working upward, or by using a drinking straw to draw out excess air before sealing.

Label all freezer bags and containers with the name of the meal, date when it was frozen, number of servings, heating instructions, and any other special preparation instructions, i.e. sprinkle with one cup grated cheese before baking.

Package grated cheese or crumb toppings in small freezer bags, tape to main dish container and include instructions on the label for adding the topping before reheating.

CHAPTER SIX

Preparing Your Kitchen

A kitchen filled with a minimum amount of high-quality, multi-use items is easier to care for than a kitchen overflowing with single-use, low quality items. The following is a list of kitchen supplies that are handy to have around for a big cooking day.

NEED TO HAVE:

apron

baking dishes (9-inch square, 9″x13″, loaf pan)

baking sheets (two)

bowls (several of various sizes for holding ingredients during preparation)

bulb baster

cake pans (two 8-inch rounds, two 8-inch squares)

can opener (high quality hand can opener or electric)

casserole dishes with covers (2 quart, 3 quart)

colander

corkscrew

cutting board

grater

hot pads (at least two)

ladles (at least two)

kitchen scissors

kitchen towels (several)

knives (8-inch chef knife, paring knife, long serrated bread knife)

measuring cups (2 complete sets— one for dry, one for wet ingredients)

measuring spoons (two complete sets)

mixing bowls (set of three: small, medium and large)

muffin tins

pastry brush

pie pans

rolling pin

rubber gloves

rubber spatulas (assorted sizes)

saucepans (one large, one medium)

scrub brush

skillets (one large, one medium)

slotted spoons (made of reinforced nylon so they won't scratch pans)

soup pan with lid (larger the better, preferably more than one)

spoons (several wooden spoons; and also several long handled stirring spoons)

tongs

vegetable peeler
vegetable steamer (wire basket that
    fits inside covered saucepan)
waterproof marking pen (Sharpie™
    brand is best)
wire whisks (set of at least two
    different sizes)

NICE TO HAVE
  (BUT NOT NECESSARY):
blender
electric mixer (hand-held or free-
    standing)
electric skillet (frees up space on
    your stovetop burners)
electric wok
food processor
garlic press
ice cream scoop (for making
    meatballs and scooping cookie
    dough)

microwave oven
pizza pan
rice cooker
salad shooter (for grating cheese)
slow cooker (having two can be
    helpful)
tea kettle (for boiling water)
toaster
toaster oven

ODDS AND ENDS:
cupcake liners
foil (heavy-duty)
freezer bags (assorted sizes)
napkins
paper towels
permanent marking pens
plastic freezer containers (in various
    sizes)
plastic wrap, clear
waxed paper

PANTRY SUPPLIES:
(Don't run out and buy all these items in one shopping trip. As you go through
your regular shopping and cooking processes, you'll find you've stocked many of
these items. If you add one or two additional items to your shopping list each
payday, you'll quickly develop a well-stocked pantry.)

allspice
almonds (whole, sliced and
    slivered)
almond extract
artichoke hearts, marinated
artichoke hearts, plain
baking chocolate (unsweetened)
baking mix (such as Bisquick™)
baking powder
baking soda
basil
bay leaves
beans (canned and dried—black,
    kidney, pinto, white and lentils)
beef broth, canned

bouillon cubes or granules (chicken
    and beef)
bread crumbs
cashews
catsup
cayenne
celery seed
chicken (canned)
chicken broth, canned
chili powder
chili sauce
chocolate chips, semi-sweet
cilantro
cinnamon, ground
cinnamon, sticks

cloves, ground
cloves, whole
cocoa powder (unsweetened)
coconut, shredded
cooking oil
cooking spray
couscous
cornmeal
cornstarch
corn syrup
crackers (assorted)
croutons
cumin
currants, dried
curry powder
dill
dry milk
egg noodles
evaporated milk
fennel
flour
fruit (canned peaches, pears,
  oranges, applesauce, mixed fruit)
garlic, minced
garlic powder
garlic salt
gelatin and pudding mixes
ginger
gravy mix packets
green chilies
herb blend
honey
hot chocolate mix, instant
Italian seasoning
jams and jellies, assorted
lemon peel
lemon juice
lemon pepper
lime juice
mace, ground
maple extract
maple syrup

marjoram
mayonnaise
mint extract
mushrooms, canned (whole and
  sliced)
mustard (regular and Dijon-style)
mustard, dry
nutmeg
nuts (walnuts, almonds, pecans)
oatmeal, instant
oats, rolled
olive oil
olives, black (whole and sliced)
olives, green
onion powder
onion salt
oregano
paprika
Parmesan cheese
parsley flakes
pastas, assorted dry (spaghetti,
  fettuccine, manicotti shells, elbow
  macaroni, bow-ties, penne,
  rigatoni, small shells, large shells)
peanut butter
peanuts, in shell
peanuts, shelled
pectin
pepper, black
pepper, white
peppercorns, whole
pepper sauce (Tabasco)
pine nuts
pizza sauce
poppy seeds
powdered milk
raisins
red pepper flakes
rice, brown
rice, instant
rice, long grain
rice, white

rice, wild
rosemary
saffron
sage
salad dressing, mix packets
salsa
salt
sesame oil
sesame seeds
Sloppy Joe seasoning packets
soup, canned (tomato, chicken noodle, French onion, whatever else your family eats regularly)
soup, cream of (mushroom, chicken, broccoli, asparagus)
soup, dry mixes (chicken noodle, French onion)
soy sauce
spaghetti sauce, jars or cans
spaghetti sauce, mix packets
sunflower seeds, shelled
sugar, brown
sugar, powdered
sugar, white
sweetened condensed milk
taco seasoning packets
tarragon
texturized vegetable protein (TVP)
tomato juice
tomato paste
tomato sauce
tomatoes, crushed or diced
tomatoes, stewed (regular, diced, Italian-style and Mexican-style)
tomatoes, with green chilies
thyme
tuna
turmeric
vanilla extract
vegetables (assorted canned)
vegetable oil
vegetable shortening (solid)

vegetable broth, canned
vegetable soup mix packets
vinegar, balsamic
vinegar, cider
vinegar, red wine
vinegar, white
vinegar, white wine
walnuts (halves and chopped)
water chestnuts
wheat germ
wine, dry red
wine, dry white
Worcestershire sauce
yeast, active dry

REFRIGERATOR & FREEZER SUPPLIES:
butter
buttermilk
cheeses (cheddar, Monterey Jack, mozzarella, Parmesan, ricotta, Romano, Swiss)
corn kernels, frozen
cottage cheese
cream, whipping
cream cheese
eggs
egg substitute
garlic cloves, whole
ginger root, whole
green beans, frozen
lemon juice
lima beans, frozen
lime juice
margarine
milk
mixed vegetables, frozen
Parmesan cheese
peas, frozen
salad dressings (assorted)
sour cream
tortillas, corn
tortillas, flour
yogurt, plain

PRODUCE:
cabbage
carrots
celery
cilantro, fresh
garlic cloves
green onions

bell pepper, green
bell pepper, red
onions
parsley, fresh
potatoes
tofu

Chicken Mini-Session #1

Chicken Fried Rice
Chicken Tortellini Soup
Lemon Mushroom Chicken

Chicken Taco Sandwiches
Chicken Chili Mac

Shopping List

MEAT
6 cups chicken (about two 3-4 lb. chickens) or 6 pounds chicken breasts
6 chicken cutlets or boneless chicken breasts

DAIRY
2 eggs
2-oz. reduced-fat cheddar cheese
⅓ cup nonfat sour cream
4-oz. reduced-fat Monterey Jack cheese
margarine

BREAD / PASTA
6 French or Kaiser rolls, split
1 cup dried cheese-filled tortellini, uncooked
6-oz. elbow macaroni, dry

VEGETABLES
3 medium onions
11 garlic cloves
fresh ginger root
1 medium zucchini
1 medium red bell pepper
1 medium green bell pepper
1 cup fresh snow peas
9 fresh asparagus spears
3 large carrots
2 celery ribs
1 head iceberg lettuce
3 medium tomatoes

1 small bunch fresh parsley

CANNED / BOXED
12-oz. long grain rice
84-oz. canned fat-free chicken broth
⅓ cup salsa (medium or hot, to taste)
2 (15-oz.) cans Mexican-style stewed tomatoes
1 (6-oz.) can red kidney beans

SPICES
cayenne
red pepper flakes
soy sauce
thyme
black pepper
bay leaf
white pepper
oregano
chili powder
sugar
cumin
flour

FROZEN
1 cup frozen corn kernels

MISC.
spray on oil
sesame oil
olive oil
lemon juice
dry white table wine

Preparation Instructions

CHICKEN PREP:

6 chicken breasts, uncooked—pound to ¼-inch thickness; keep covered in refrigerator until ready to use.

3 cups cooked chicken breasts—cut into ½-inch pieces.

3 cups cooked chicken breasts—shred.

To prepare, boil chicken pieces in a large Dutch oven or stock pot with enough water to fully cover the chicken. Add several stalks of celery and some sliced onion, if desired. Boil until meat is white to the bone and falling off the bone easily. After the chicken is finished cooking, cool slightly and place the pot in the refrigerator to cool completely overnight. The fat will congeal on top of the pot so you can easily scoop it away in the morning. After you've scooped off the fat, remove the chicken from the broth and de-bone. Save the broth from the cooked chicken for using in recipes or making soup.

VEGETABLE PREP:

3 medium onions—chop.

1 medium zucchini—slice into ½-inch pieces

1 cup green bell pepper—chop.

1 cup red bell pepper—chop coarsely.

1 cup snow peas—remove stem ends and strings; cut into 1-inch pieces.

1 cup carrots—slice thinly.

½ cup celery—slice thinly.

2 cups fresh mushrooms—slice.

9 asparagus spears—cut into ½-inch pieces.

11 garlic cloves—mince.

2 teaspoon fresh ginger root—pare and mince.

CHEESE PREP:

4-oz. (1 cup) reduced-fat Monterey Jack cheese—grate.

ODDS AND ENDS PREP:

12-oz. long-grain white rice—cook according to package directions.

6-oz. elbow macaroni—cook according to package directions. Set in large pan of cold water; store in refrigerator until ready to use.

Note: Place vegetables, meats and cheese into separate covered bowls or plastic bags and refrigerate until ready to use.

Chicken Fried Rice

6 servings

12-oz. long-grain white rice

2 tablespoons oriental sesame oil

2 cups chicken breasts, cooked and cut into ½-inch pieces

1½ cup onion, chopped finely

2 teaspoons fresh ginger root, pared and minced

3 garlic cloves, minced

⅛ teaspoon red pepper flakes, crushed

1 medium zucchini, slice into ½-inch pieces

1 cup red bell pepper, chopped coarsely

1 cup snow peas, stem ends and strings removed; cut into 1-inch pieces

9 asparagus spears, cut into ½-inch pieces

2 eggs, beaten

5 tablespoons soy sauce

ADVANCED PREP:

Cook chicken in large pot of water the night before. Cut cooked chicken into ½-inch pieces. Cook rice the night before. Store chicken and rice in separate containers in the refrigerator until ready to prepare. Chop onions and red bell pepper. Mince ginger root and garlic. Slice zucchini into ½-inch pieces. Remove strings from snow peas and cut into 1-inch pieces. Cut asparagus spears into ½-inch pieces.

PREPARATION:

Cook onions, ginger, garlic and pepper flakes in 1½ tablespoons sesame oil. Cook over medium-high heat for two minutes. Add zucchini, bell pepper, snow peas and asparagus. Cook, stirring frequently 3 - 4 minutes or until vegetables are just softened. In separate pan, scramble eggs. Stir eggs, chicken and vegetable mixture into rice. Stir in soy sauce. Put into labeled freezer bag; seal and freeze.

TO SERVE:

Thaw. Heat in medium-hot skillet with 2 teaspoons oil. Cook stirring constantly 5 minutes, or until heated through.

PER SERVING: 428 CALORIES; 9.0G FAT; 28.2G PROTEIN; 58.3G CARBOHYDRATES; 120MG CHOLESTEROL.

Chicken Taco Sandwiches

6 servings

2 cups shredded chicken breast
  meat
1 cup chicken broth
3 garlic cloves, minced

1 teaspoon dried oregano leaves
1 teaspoon ground cumin
⅓ cup medium or hot salsa
Six French or Kaiser rolls, split

For Serving Day •
(purchase when needed if not eating within 2 or 3 days):

3 cups shredded iceberg lettuce
  leaves
3 medium tomatoes, diced

2-oz. (½ cup) reduced-fat
  cheddar cheese, grated
⅓ cup nonfat sour cream

ADVANCED PREP:

Cook chicken the night before. Shred chicken meat. Mince garlic cloves.

PREPARATION:

Boil 1 cup chicken broth with garlic, oregano and cumin until reduced to ⅓
cup. Stir into shredded chicken meat with the salsa. Place in labeled freezer bag.
Freeze. Wrap rolls in foil, label and freeze.

TO SERVE:

Thaw. Reheat in microwave or saucepan until hot. Serve in French or Kaiser
rolls with hot chicken mixture, shredded lettuce, chopped tomatoes, grated
cheese and sour cream for garnish.

PER SERVING: 278.0 CALORIES; 7.3G FAT; 24.7G PROTEIN; 25.6G CARBOHYDRATES; 56MG CHOLESTEROL.

Chicken Tortellini Soup

6 servings

1 cup carrots, sliced thinly
½ cup onion, chopped
½ cup celery, sliced thinly
1 cup chicken breasts, cut into ½-inch cubes
6 cups reduced-fat chicken broth (reserved from cooking chicken or canned)

1 cup cheese-filled tortellini, dried and uncooked
½ teaspoon thyme leaves, dried
¼ teaspoon black pepper
1 bay leaf
2 tablespoons fresh parsley, snipped

ADVANCE PREP:

Cook chicken the night before; reserve broth. Cut into ½-inch cubes. Slice carrots and celery. Chop onion.

PREPARATION:

Use broth reserved from cooking chicken the night before. Bring broth to a boil, add carrots, onion, celery, thyme, black pepper and bay leaf. Cover; simmer over medium-low heat for 15 minutes. Cool. Remove bay leaf. Add chicken, pasta and parsley. Place in labeled freezer bags; seal and freeze.

TO SERVE:

Thaw. Reheat over medium heat, covered, for 15 minutes or until pasta is cooked.

PER SERVING: 121.6 CALORIES; 3.8G FAT; 20.0G PROTEIN; 11.5G CARBOHYDRATES; 29MG CHOLESTEROL.

Chicken Chili Mac

6 servings

6-oz. elbow macaroni, dry

7-oz. skinless chicken breasts, cooked and shredded

1 cup chicken broth

1 cup onions, chopped

1 cup green bell peppers, chopped

2 tablespoons chili powder

2 garlic cloves, minced

¾ teaspoon cumin

½ teaspoon oregano

¼ teaspoon sugar

¼ teaspoon cayenne

2 (15-oz.) cans Mexican-style stewed tomatoes, chopped (undrained)

1 cup frozen corn kernels, thawed

1 (6-oz.) can red kidney beans, drained

4-oz. (1 cup) reduced fat Monterey Jack cheese, grated (reserve ¼ cup)

ADVANCE PREP:

Cook chicken night before. Shred chicken. Cook noodles until just barely tender. Drain noodles; rinse in cold water; set in large pan of cold water; store in refrigerator until ready to use. Chop onion and green bell pepper. Grate Monterey Jack cheese. Mince garlic.

PREPARATION:

In small saucepan, heat 1 cup chicken broth. Cook onion and green pepper in broth until soft. Add chili powder, garlic, cumin, oregano, sugar and cayenne. Cook, stirring constantly, 1 minute. Remove from heat. Add tomatoes, corn and beans. Stir in drained macaroni. Stir in chicken and cheese (reserve ¼ cup cheese). Place in labeled freezer bag. Place reserved cheese in separate labeled freezer bag. Tape bags together or place both bags together into another freezer bag. Seal and freeze.

TO SERVE:

Thaw. Pour into casserole dish. Sprinkle with reserved cheese. Bake 25 minutes at 350 degrees.

PER SERVING: 323.2 CALORIES; 6.8G FAT; 32.1 PROTEIN; 33.4 CARBOHYDRATES; 58MG CHOLESTEROL.

Lemon Mushroom Chicken

6 servings

6 chicken breasts, pounded to ¼-inch thickness

9 tablespoons flour

3 teaspoons margarine

3 teaspoons olive oil

2 cups fresh mushrooms, sliced

3 garlic cloves, minced

1½ cups reduced-fat chicken broth

6 tablespoons lemon juice

6 tablespoons dry white table wine

3 teaspoons parsley

½ teaspoon white pepper

ADVANCE PREP:

Pound 6 chicken breasts to ¼-inch thickness. Slice mushrooms. Mince garlic.

PREPARATION:

On sheet of wax paper or paper plate dredge pounded chicken breasts in flour, lightly coating both sides and reserving remaining flour. In 10-inch nonstick skillet combine margarine and oil and heat until margarine is melted; add chicken and cook over medium-high heat, turning once, until lightly browned, 2 - 3 minutes on each side. Transfer chicken to plate and set aside. In same skillet combine mushrooms and garlic and sauté over medium-high heat, until mushrooms are softened, 1 - 2 minutes. Sprinkle with reserved flour and stir quickly to combine; stir in remaining ingredients and bring to a boil. Reduce heat to low and let simmer, stirring frequently, until mixture thickens and flavors blend, 3 - 4 minutes. Return chicken to skillet and cook until heated through, 1 - 2 minutes. Remove from heat. Cool. Place in labeled freezer bag; pour mushroom sauce over chicken. Seal and freeze.

TO SERVE:

Thaw. Place chicken and mushroom sauce into non-stick skillet. Heat over medium heat until heated through. Serve.

PER SERVING: 168.6 CALORIES; 6.0G FAT; 12.2G PROTEIN; 15.2G CARBOHYDRATES; 18MG CHOLESTEROL.

Chicken Mini-Session #2

White Chicken Chili
Chicken-Asparagus Crustless Quiche
Cacciatore Penne
Marinated Lime Chicken
Cheddar Chicken

Shopping List

MEAT
7 pounds boneless chicken breasts
6 whole chicken breast portions
3 slices bacon

DAIRY
2½ cups skim milk
3 eggs
10-oz. reduced-fat cheddar cheese
Parmesan cheese

BREAD / PASTA
egg noodles to serve six
10-oz. (2 cups) uncooked penne
   pasta

VEGETABLES
8 large asparagus spears
1 medium red bell pepper
1 medium green bell pepper
3 medium onions
5 limes
1 bunch green onions
1 large tomato
4 garlic cloves

one bunch fresh cilantro
½ pound whole mushrooms

CANNED / BOXED
32-oz. fat-free chicken broth
24-oz. canned white beans
2 (4.5 ounce) cans chopped mild
   green chilies
2 (14.5-oz.) can diced tomatoes
   with Italian seasonings,
   undrained

SPICES
salt
pepper
cayenne
basil
cumin
flour

MISC.
vegetable oil
olive oil
white wine vinegar

Preparation Instructions

CHICKEN PREP:

6 whole portions chicken breasts—leave these *whole and uncooked*; store in refrigerator until ready to use.

6 pounds chicken breasts—cooked and cubed. To prepare, boil chicken pieces in a large Dutch oven or stock pot with enough water to fully cover the chicken. Add several stalks of celery and some sliced onion, if desired. Boil until meat is white to the bone and falling off the bone easily. After the chicken is finished cooking, cool slightly and place the pot in refrigerator to cool completely overnight. The fat will congeal on top of the pot so you can easily scoop it away in the morning. After you've scooped off the fat, remove the chicken from the broth and de-bone. Save the broth from the cooked chicken for using in recipes or making soup.

VEGETABLE PREP:

3 medium onions—chop.
2 cups asparagus—cut into 1-inch pieces.
1 green bell pepper—slice thinly.
½ cup red bell pepper—chop finely.
¼ cup green onion—slice.
1 tomato—seed and dice.
4 garlic cloves—mince.
5 limes—squeeze juice.
¼ cup fresh cilantro—chop coarsely.
1 (8-oz.) package whole mushrooms—halve.

CHEESE PREP:

10-oz. reduced-fat cheddar cheese—grate.

ODDS AND ENDS PREP:

3 slices bacon—cook and crumble.
1⅓ cups uncooked penne pasta—cook according to package directions until just tender. Rinse in cold water; place in large pan of cold water; store in refrigerator until ready to use.

Note: Place vegetables, meats and cheese into separate covered bowls or plastic bags and refrigerate until ready to use.

White Chicken Chili

6 servings

24-oz. canned white beans
2 cups chicken breasts, cubed
1 cup reduced-fat chicken broth
2 medium onions, chopped
4 garlic cloves, minced
2 (4-oz.) cans chopped mild
  green chilies

1 teaspoon cumin
1½ teaspoon cayenne
juice of one lime
¼ cup fresh cilantro, chopped
  coarsely

ADVANCE PREP:

Cook chicken meat; cut into ½-inch cubes. Chop onions. Mince garlic.

PREPARATION:

In skillet, combine broth, onions and garlic. Heat to boiling and cook until onions are softened. Remove from heat and cool. While onions cook, combine in a large bowl the chicken meat, canned beans, canned chilies, cumin and cayenne. Gently stir in cooled onion/broth mixture. Place in labeled freezer bag. Seal and freeze. In small freezer bag, combine lime juice and cilantro. Label, attach to chili bag or place all bags together into another freezer bag and freeze together.

TO SERVE:

Thaw both bags completely. In large saucepan, heat the contents of the chili bag until heated through. Just before serving, stir in lime juice and cilantro mixture.
PER SERVING: 277.0 CALORIES; 3.2G FAT; 29.1G PROTEIN; 33.8G CARBOHYDRATES; 49MG CHOLESTEROL.

Chicken-Asparagus Crustless Quiche

6 servings

2 cups asparagus, cut into 1-inch pieces

2 tablespoons flour

½ teaspoon salt

¼ teaspoon black pepper

pinch cayenne

1 cup chicken breast meat, cooked and cubed

2 teaspoons vegetable oil

½ cup red bell pepper, chopped finely

½ cup onion, chopped

1 cup skim milk

3 eggs (or one cup egg substitute)

4-oz. (1 cup) reduced-fat cheddar cheese, grated

ADVANCE PREP:

Cook chicken; cut into ½-inch pieces. Chop bell pepper and onion. Cut asparagus spears into 1-inch pieces. Grate cheese.

PREPARATION:

Cook asparagus just until tender. Drain; rinse. In skillet, heat oil over medium-high heat. Cook red bell pepper and onion 5 minutes or until soft. Remove from heat. Stir in chicken, salt, pepper and cayenne. In large bowl, whisk together milk, eggs and 2 tablespoons flour until frothy. Stir in cheese, asparagus and chicken/vegetable mixture. Stir to combine. Pour into labeled freezer bag; seal and freeze.

TO SERVE:

Thaw completely. Squeeze bag gently to recombine quiche mixture. Preheat oven to 350 degrees. Spray 9-inch pie plate or quiche pan with cooking spray. Pour quiche mixture into pie plate. Bake 45 minutes, or until knife inserted near center comes out clean. Let stand 10 minutes before serving. Slice into six equal wedge shaped servings.

PER SERVING: 173.6 CALORIES; 6.7G FAT; 19.6G PROTEIN; 8.5G CARBOHYDRATES; 136MG CHOLESTEROL.

Cacciatore Penne

6 servings

2 cups chicken breast meat,
  cooked and cubed

1 cup canned reduced-fat
  chicken broth

1 small green bell pepper,
  thinly sliced

1 (8-oz.) package whole
  mushrooms, halved

2 (14.5-oz.) cans diced
  tomatoes with Italian
  seasonings, undrained

10-oz. (2 cups) uncooked penne
  pasta

¼ cup Parmesan cheese (for
  serving day)

ADVANCE PREP:

Cook chicken; cut into cubes. Slice green pepper. Halve mushrooms. Cook
pasta according to package directions until just tender. Rinse in cold water;
place in large pan of cold water; store in refrigerator until ready to use.

PREPARATION:

In large skillet combine broth, sliced green bell pepper, mushrooms and
tomatoes. Cook over medium-high heat until green pepper slices are tender and
mushrooms are cooked through. Remove from heat. Stir in chicken and drained
pasta. Pour into labeled freezer bag; seal and freeze.

TO SERVE:

Thaw completely. Reheat in large skillet until heated through. Serve hot,
sprinkled with Parmesan cheese.

PER SERVING: 320 CALORIES; 3.3G FAT; 26.0G PROTEIN; 47.1G CARBOHYDRATES; 40MG CHOLESTEROL.

Marinated Lime Chicken

6 servings

6 chicken breast portions
  (about 8-oz. each)
½ teaspoon salt
¼ teaspoon pepper

4 limes (or 4 tablespoons
  bottled lime juice)
4 teaspoons white wine vinegar
9 tablespoons olive oil
2 teaspoons basil

ADVANCE PREP:

None required for this recipe.

PREPARATION:

Squeeze limes into a medium sized bowl. Stir in vinegar, olive oil, basil, salt and pepper. Place chicken breast portions into labeled freezer bag. Pour lime sauce over top; seal and freeze.

TO SERVE:

Thaw completely. Pour marinade into small saucepan. Heat to boiling. Place chicken pieces into shallow oven-proof dish. Pour boiled marinade over chicken. Bake in preheated 350 degree oven for 35 - 40 minutes or until chicken is tender and cooked through. Serve hot, sprinkled with fresh basil sprigs if available.

PER SERVING: 191.8 CALORIES; 4.1G FAT; 32.8G PROTEIN; 6.2G CARBOHYDRATES; 81MG CHOLESTEROL.

Cheddar Chicken

6 servings

1½ cups skim milk
1½ cups canned fat-free chicken broth
3 tablespoons flour
6-oz. reduced-fat cheddar cheese, grated
2 cups cooked chicken, cut into ½-inch cubes

¼ cup green onions, sliced
½ cup tomato, seeded and diced
3 slices bacon, cooked and crumbled
egg noodles to serve six

ADVANCE PREP:

Cook chicken; cut into ½-inch cubes. Slice green onions. Cook and crumble bacon. Seed and dice tomato. Grate cheddar cheese.

PREPARATION:

In large saucepan, mix together milk, broth and flour. Heat over medium heat, stirring constantly until sauce thickens. Add cheese. Stir until melted. Add chicken pieces, green onions, tomatoes and bacon. Cool. Pour into labeled freezer bags; seal and freeze.

TO SERVE:

Thaw completely. Reheat in saucepan over medium-low heat until heated through. Serve over hot cooked noodles.

PER SERVING: 349.3 CALORIES; 5.0G FAT; 29.0G PROTEIN; 48.0G CARBOHYDRATES; 94MG CHOLESTEROL.

Chicken Session #3

Cheese and Chicken Shells *Spiced Chicken Sandwiches*
Artichoke Chicken Bake *Chicken Enchiladas*
Chicken Mushroom Rolls *Chicken Broccoli Noodles*

Shopping List

MEAT
24 boneless chicken breast halves

DAIRY
3 eggs
1¾ cups skim milk
fat-free mayonnaise
3 cups fat-free sour cream
margarine
½ cup fat-free cottage cheese (or Ricotta)
2-oz. reduced-fat mozzarella cheese, grated
4-oz. reduced-fat Swiss cheese
3-oz. package fat-free cream cheese
4-oz. reduced-fat cheddar cheese

BREAD / PASTA
12 jumbo shell macaroni
6 soft sandwich rolls, split
6 (6-inch) flour tortillas
10-oz. uncooked wide egg noodles

VEGETABLES
2 large carrots
4 garlic cloves
3 medium tomatoes
1 red onion
1 small green pepper
2 medium onions
2 celery ribs
1 bunch green onions
1 bunch fresh cilantro

3 cups broccoli florettes
2 cups sliced mushrooms

CANNED / BOXED
4 ½ cups fat-free chicken broth
1 (14-oz.) can artichoke hearts, drained and halved (not the marinated type)
½ cup salsa (medium or hot, according to taste)
1 (10¾ oz.) can 98% fat-free cream of chicken soup
2-oz. onion and garlic flavored croutons

SPICES
flour
cornstarch
nutmeg
cumin
parsley
garlic powder
salt
pepper
thyme
paprika
cayenne
½ cup sliced almonds
MISC.
1¼ cups dry white wine (or apple juice)
vegetable oil
lemon juice

Preparation Instructions

CHICKEN PREP:

6 whole *uncooked* chicken breast portions—pound breasts with meat mallet until very thin.

6 whole *cooked* chicken breast portions—leave these whole after cooking. To prepare, boil chicken pieces in a large Dutch oven or stock pot with enough water to fully cover the chicken. Add several stalks of celery and some sliced onion, if desired. Boil until meat is white to the bone and falling off the bone easily. After the chicken is finished cooking, cool slightly and place the pot in the refrigerator to cool completely overnight. The fat will congeal on top of the pot so you can easily scoop it away in the morning. After you've scooped off the fat, remove the chicken from the broth and de-bone. Save the broth from the cooked chicken for using in recipes or making soup.

3 cups of cooked chicken meat—shred.

2 cups of cooked chicken meat—cut into strips.

rest of cooked chicken meat—chop in ½-inch pieces.

VEGETABLE PREP:

1½ cups onion—chop.

½ cup green onions—slice thinly.

½ cup carrot—grate.

½ cup celery—chop.

½ cup green bell pepper—chop.

4 garlic cloves—mince.

¼ cup fresh cilantro—mince.

3 cups fresh broccoli—cut into bite-sized pieces; steam until just tender; rinse with cold water.

2 cups fresh mushrooms—slice.

CHEESE PREP:

2-oz. (½ cup) reduced-fat Mozzarella cheese—grate.

4-oz. (1 cup) reduced-fat Swiss cheese—grate.

4-oz. (1 cup) reduced-fat cheddar cheese—grate.

ODDS AND ENDS PREP:

12 jumbo shell macaroni—cook according to package directions. Rinse in cold water to stop cooking process. Place in large pan of water in refrigerator until ready to use.

Cheese and Chicken Shells

6 servings

12 jumbo shell macaroni
1 egg, beaten
½ cup fat-free cottage cheese
  (or fat-free Ricotta)
1 cup cooked chicken, shredded
2-oz. (½ cup) reduced-fat
  mozzarella cheese, grated
½ cup carrot, grated
1 clove garlic, minced

¼ teaspoon salt
pepper to taste
1¾ cups skim milk
2 tablespoons cornstarch
4-oz. (1 cup) reduced-fat Swiss
  cheese, grated
⅛ teaspoon nutmeg

ADVANCE PREP:

Cook chicken; shred (for total of 1 cup). Cook macaroni shells according to package directions. Rinse in cold water to stop the cooking process. Grate mozzarella and Swiss cheeses. Grate carrots.

PREPARATION:

In mixing bowl, combine beaten egg, cottage cheese, chicken, mozzarella cheese, grated carrot, garlic, salt and pepper. Spoon into cooked pasta shells. In medium saucepan, combine milk and cornstarch; cook and stir until thickened and bubbly. Add Swiss cheese and nutmeg. Stir until cheese is melted. Place stuffed shells into freezer-safe pan. Spoon sauce evenly over shells. Cover with foil; label and freeze.

TO SERVE:

Thaw. Bake in 350 degree oven for ½ hour or until heated through. Sprinkle with a small amount of nutmeg.

PER SERVING: 341 CALORIES; 4.5G FAT; 21.7G PROTEIN; 52.0 CARBOHYDRATES; 51MG CHOLESTEROL.

Spiced Chicken Sandwiches

6 servings

Six soft rolls, split
½ teaspoon cumin
½ teaspoon garlic powder
½ teaspoon salt
½ teaspoon pepper
½ teaspoon thyme
¼ teaspoon paprika
pinch cayenne

16-oz. skinless boneless chicken breast, cooked and cut into strips
¼ cup fat-free mayonnaise
1 cup reduced-fat chicken broth

For serving day:
2 medium tomatoes, sliced
½ cup red onion, sliced thinly

ADVANCED PREP:

Cook chicken breasts in stockpot; cool and cut into strips.

PREPARATION:

Stir cumin, garlic powder, salt, black pepper, thyme, paprika and cayenne into ¼ cup fat-free mayonnaise. Place chicken slices into labeled freezer bag; pour chicken broth over chicken strips; seal. Place mayonnaise/spice mixture into small freezer-safe covered bowl. Into large freezer bag, place chicken bag, mayonnaise container and rolls. Freeze.

TO SERVE:

Thaw. Heat chicken slices and broth in large skillet until heated through. Pour off excess broth. While chicken is heating, slice tomatoes and red onion. Assemble sandwiches by spreading split rolls with mayonnaise/spice mixture. Divide chicken evenly between rolls. Layer with tomato and onion slices and top with other half of roll. Serve warm.

PER SERVING: 201.2 CALORIES; 2.5G FAT; 19.7G PROTEIN; 25.6G CARBOHYDRATES; 35MG CHOLESTEROL.

Artichoke Chicken Bake

6 servings

¼ cup butter or margarine
6 boneless, skinless chicken
  breasts
1 cup onion, chopped
1 garlic clove, minced
2 tablespoons flour
¼ teaspoon salt

1¼ cup dry white wine (or
  apple juice)
1 cup canned reduced-fat
  chicken broth
1 (3-oz) package fat-free cream
  cheese
1 (14-oz.) can artichoke hearts,
  drained and halved (*not*
  marinated artichoke hearts)

For Serving Day:
½ cups sliced almonds (to be added at serving time)
2 tablespoons parsley

ADVANCED PREP:

Cook chicken in stockpot. Remember to keep these six chicken pieces whole after cooking (don't cut or shred). Chop onion. Mince garlic.

PREPARATION:

Melt butter in large skillet over medium heat. Sauté onion and garlic until tender. Stir in flour and salt until smooth. Cook 1 minute, stirring constantly. Add wine (or juice) and broth; cook over medium heat, stirring constantly, until mixture is thickened and bubbly. Add cream cheese, stirring until cheese melts. Remove from heat; set aside. Place chicken breasts in 2-quart casserole dish; arrange artichoke hearts over chicken. Spoon cream cheese mixture over chicken and artichokes. Cover, label and freeze.

TO SERVE:

Thaw. Bake uncovered at 350 degrees for 35 minutes or until bubbly. Sprinkle with almonds and parsley.

PER SERVING: 382.3 CALORIES; 14.7G FAT; 41.3G PROTEIN; 15.5G CARBOHYDRATES; 82MG CHOLESTEROL.

Chicken Enchiladas

6 servings

2 cups boneless chicken breasts, shredded

2 cups fat-free sour cream

½ cup green onions, sliced thinly

¼ fresh cilantro, minced

½ teaspoon cumin

½ teaspoon salt

¼ teaspoon garlic powder

6 flour tortillas

4-oz. (1 cup) reduced-fat cheddar cheese, grated

For Serving Day:

½ cup mild or medium salsa (to taste)

½ cup tomato, chopped

fresh cilantro sprigs to garnish

ADVANCE PREP:

Cook chicken in stockpot; shred cooked chicken meat. Grate cheddar cheese. Slice green onions. Mince cilantro.

PREPARATION:

In mixing bowl, combine shredded chicken, sour cream, green onions, cilantro, cumin, salt and garlic powder. Place chicken mixture into freezer bag. In separate bag, place grated cheese. Into large labeled freezer bag, place chicken mixture bag, cheese bag and tortillas. Freeze.

TO SERVE:

Thaw. Preheat oven to 350 degrees. Spray 13x9 baking pan with cooking spray. Assemble enchiladas by placing tortillas in single layer on countertop. Divide chicken mixture evenly between the six tortillas. Fold sides of tortillas over filling; place seam-side down into baking pan. Sprinkle with grated cheese. Cover tightly; bake 25 minutes or until filling is hot and cheese is melted. Spoon salsa over enchiladas; sprinkle with chopped tomato and garnish with fresh cilantro sprigs.

PER SERVING: 261.4 CALORIES; 4.5G FAT; 24.7G PROTEIN; 31.0G CARBOHYDRATES; 40MG CHOLESTEROL.

Chicken Mushroom Rolls

6 servings

2 cups mushrooms, sliced
4 teaspoons margarine
4 teaspoons flour
1 cup reduced-fat chicken broth
1 teaspoon lemon juice
½ cup onion, chopped
½ cup celery, chopped

½ cup green bell pepper, chopped
2 garlic cloves, minced
2-oz. onion and garlic-flavored croutons
2 eggs, beaten
6 boneless chicken breasts, pounded thin

ADVANCE PREP:

Pound chicken breasts with meat mallet until very thin. Chop onion, celery and green pepper. Slice mushrooms. Mince garlic.

PREPARATION:

In large skillet, melt ½ the margarine (2 teaspoons). Add onion, celery, green pepper and garlic; sauté until softened. Remove from heat. In another skillet, melt 2 teaspoons margarine. Stir in mushrooms and cook until softened, stirring frequently. Sprinkle flour over mushrooms; stir to combine. Stir constantly over medium heat for 1 minute. Add broth and lemon juice to mushrooms. Cook for 2 minutes, stirring frequently. Remove from heat. Stir croutons and beaten eggs into onion/celery/green pepper mixture. Spread vegetable/crouton mixture onto center of each pounded chicken breast. Roll chicken breast around filling. Secure each chicken roll with a toothpick and place seam-side down in 9x13-inch baking dish. Cover, label and freeze. Pour mushroom sauce into labeled freezer bag; attach to chicken roll pan; freeze.

TO SERVE:

Thaw. Stir mushroom sauce to recombine. Add a small amount of water or chicken broth if too thick. Pour mushroom sauce over top of chicken rolls. Tightly cover pan and bake at 350 degrees for 45 minutes until chicken is cooked through.

PER SERVING: 284.1 CALORIES; 8.1G FAT; 39.5G PROTEIN; 13.8G CARBOHYDRATES; 153MG CHOLESTEROL.

Chicken Broccoli Noodles

6 servings

6 boneless skinless chicken
  breasts, cut into ½-inch
  pieces
3 cups fresh broccoli florettes
10-oz. (3½ cups) wide egg
  noodles, dry

1½ cups canned fat-free
  chicken broth
1½ cups water
1 cup non-fat sour cream
1 (10 ¾-oz.) can 98% fat-free
  cream of chicken soup

ADVANCE PREP:

Cook chicken in stockpot. Cut into ½-inch pieces. Cut up broccoli and steam
until just tender. Rinse with cold water.

PREPARATION:

In medium mixing bowl, combine chicken broth, water, sour cream and
chicken soup. In large bowl, place chicken pieces and broccoli. Pour soup and
water mixture over top. Stir gently to combine. Pour into large freezer bag, label
and freeze.

TO SERVE:

Thaw. Reheat in skillet over medium heat, stirring frequently. Serve over hot,
cooked egg noodles.

PER SERVING: 387.7CALORIES; 4.4G FAT; 46.1G PROTEIN; 41.8G CARBOHYDRATES; 132MG CHOLESTEROL.

Chicken Session #4

Old-fashioned Chicken and Rice
Chicken Vegetable Skillet
Chicken Pasta Italiano
Chicken Noodle Soup
Mushroom Chicken Couscous

Shopping List

MEAT
6 pounds boneless, skinless chicken
  breasts

DAIRY
margarine
Parmesan cheese
2 cups skim milk

BREAD / PASTA
1½ cups long grain white rice
6-oz. bow tie pasta
5-oz. wide egg noodles
1 ½ cups couscous

VEGETABLES
6 large onions
1 bunch fresh parsley
14 garlic cloves
1 small green bell pepper
2 small red bell pepper
fresh cilantro
4 large carrots
1 large celery rib
1 pound potatoes
3 medium tomatoes
2 small zucchini
12-oz. mushrooms, sliced

CANNED / BOXED
92-oz. (11½ cups) canned fat-free
  chicken broth
1 (6-oz.) jar sliced mushrooms
1 (16-oz.) can Italian-style stewed
  tomatoes

SPICES
poultry seasonings
thyme
salt
pepper
Italian seasoning
cornstarch
cayenne

FROZEN
½ cup frozen
  peas

MISC.
olive oil
vegetable oil
cooking spray
cooking sherry
soy sauce
white vinegar

Preparation Instructions

CHICKEN PREP:

4½ pounds boneless, skinless chicken breasts—cut into
1-inch cubes.

1 pound chicken breasts—slice into ½-inch strips.

1 pound chicken breasts—place between sheets of plastic wrap or wax paper;
pound with meat mallet until ¼-inch thick; cut into ½-inch wide strips.

VEGETABLE PREP:

6 cups onions—chop.

½ cup celery—chop.

3 medium-sized tomatoes—seed and chop.

½ cup fresh parsley—chop.

1 small green pepper—chop.

2 small zucchini—slice thinly.

4 large carrots—slice thinly.

½ pound fresh mushrooms—slice.

2 small red bell peppers—cut into strips.

14 garlic cloves—mince

1 pound potatoes, peeled and thinly sliced. Place potatoes in a large bowl of
cold water with 1 teaspoon white vinegar or lemon juice. Refrigerate until
ready to use; dry thoroughly before adding to skillet when preparing recipe.

Old-Fashioned Chicken and Rice

6 servings

2½ cups canned fat-free
  chicken broth

1½ pounds boneless skinless
  chicken breasts, cut into 1-
  inch pieces

1½ cups long-grain rice,
  uncooked

1 cup onions, chopped

¼ cup fresh parsley, minced

6 garlic cloves, minced

1 small red bell pepper, sliced
  into thin strips

1 (6-oz.) jar sliced mushrooms,
  undrained

1 teaspoon poultry seasonings

ADVANCED PREP:

Cut up chicken into 1-inch pieces. Chop onions. Mince garlic cloves and
parsley. Slice red bell pepper into long thin strips.

PREPARATION:

In large saucepan or Dutch oven, bring broth to a boil. Add remaining
ingredients. Mix well and return to boil. Reduce heat to medium; cover tightly
and cook 20 minutes or until chicken is no longer pink and rice is tender. Cool.
Place into labeled freezer bags; freeze.

TO SERVE:

Thaw. Place into large skillet; heat over medium heat until heated through.
Serve.

PER SERVING: 301.9 CALORIES; 1.7G FAT; 30.2G PROTEIN; 43.3G CARBOHYDRATES; 53MG CHOLESTEROL.

Chicken Vegetable Skillet

6 servings

6 teaspoons olive oil or
vegetable oil

1 pound potatoes, sliced thinly

1 pound boneless chicken
breasts, cut into 1-inch cubes

3 tablespoons butter or
margarine

1 cup onion, chopped

1 cup green bell pepper,
chopped

1 cup carrot, sliced

3 garlic cloves, minced

1 (15-oz.) can Italian-style
stewed tomatoes (with liquid)

3 tablespoons fresh parsley,
chopped

½ teaspoon thyme

½ teaspoon salt

½ teaspoon pepper

1 teaspoon white vinegar or
lemon juice

ADVANCE PREP:

Cut chicken into 1-inch cubes. Chop onion and green pepper. Slice carrots.
Mince garlic. Peel and thinly slice potatoes; place potatoes in a large bowl of
cold water with 1 teaspoon white vinegar or lemon juice. Refrigerate potatoes
until ready to use; dry thoroughly before adding to skillet. Chop stewed
tomatoes; reserve liquid.

PREPARATION:

In large skillet, heat oil over medium-high heat; add potatoes and chicken; cook
until chicken is no longer pink, stirring constantly. Transfer mixture to another
container and set aside. Using same skillet, melt butter and stir in onion, green
pepper, carrot slices and garlic; cook over high heat until just barely tender. Add
potato-chicken mixture to vegetables in skillet. Stir in tomatoes, tomato liquid
and remaining spices. Reduce heat to low and cook, stirring frequently, until
potatoes are just barely starting to get tender (less than 5 minutes). Remove
from heat. Cool in refrigerator. Place mixture into labeled freezer bag; seal and
freeze.

TO SERVE:

Thaw. Heat in large skillet over medium heat until heated through.

PER SERVING: 254.8 CALORIES; 11.3G FAT; 17.0G PROTEIN; 22.8G CARBOHYDRATES; 35MG CHOLESTEROL.

Chicken Pasta Italiano

6 servings

6-oz. bow tie pasta, uncooked
2 medium tomatoes, seeded and chopped
1 cup onion, chopped
1 small zucchini, sliced
1 small red pepper, cut into thin strips
2 teaspoons olive oil
2 garlic cloves, minced

1 pound boneless chicken breasts, cut into ½-inch strips
½ cup frozen peas
1 teaspoon salt
1 teaspoon dried Italian seasoning
⅛ cup Parmesan cheese (for serving day)

ADVANCE PREP:

Seed and chop tomatoes. Chop onion. Slice zucchini. Cut red pepper into thin strips. Mince garlic. Cut chicken breasts into ½-inch strips.

PREPARATION:

In large skillet, heat oil over medium heat. Add garlic and chicken strips; cook 5 minutes, stirring frequently. Add onion, zucchini, red pepper, frozen peas, salt and Italian seasoning. Cook 1 minute longer. Remove from heat and stir in tomatoes. Cool. Place into labeled freezer bags. Freeze.

TO SERVE:

Thaw chicken mixture. Cook bow-tie pasta according to package directions. Heat chicken mixture in large skillet over medium heat until heated through. Toss together pasta and chicken mixture; sprinkle with Parmesan cheese.

PER SERVING: 197.7 CALORIES; 3.1G FAT; 13.0G PROTEIN; 29.6G CARBOHYDRATES; 19MG CHOLESTEROL.

Chicken Noodle Soup

6 servings

1 teaspoon vegetable oil
2 cups onion, chopped
8 cups reduced-fat chicken
  broth
3 cloves garlic, minced
½ teaspoon thyme
¼ teaspoon pepper
2 large carrots, sliced thinly
½ cup celery, chopped

5-oz. dried wide egg noodles
1 pound boneless chicken
  breasts, cut into 1-inch cubes
  (about two cups)
1 small zucchini, thinly sliced
1 medium-sized tomato, seeded
  and chopped
2 tablespoons parsley, chopped

ADVANCE PREP:

Cut chicken into ½-inch cubes. Chop onions, celery and parsley. Seed and chop tomatoes. Mince garlic. Slice carrots.

PREPARATION:

In large pan or Dutch oven, heat oil over medium heat. Add onion and cook until softened, stirring frequently. Stir in broth, garlic, thyme, pepper, carrots, celery and chicken. Reduce heat to low; cover and simmer until carrots are barely tender and chicken is no longer pink (less than 10 minutes). Remove from heat. Stir in zucchini, tomato and parsley. Cool. Pour into labeled freezer bag; freeze.

TO SERVE:

Thaw. Place in large pan or Dutch oven; add noodles. Heat over medium heat until heated through and noodles are cooked through.

PER SERVING: 230.3 CALORIES; 2.9G FAT; 33.6G PROTEIN; 29.1G CARBOHYDRATES; 58MG CHOLESTEROL.

Mushroom Chicken Couscous

6 servings

1 pound skinless, boneless
  chicken breasts
1 tablespoon margarine
1 large onion, chopped finely
8-oz. mushrooms, sliced
2 teaspoons cornstarch
¼ cup reduced-fat chicken
  broth
3 tablespoons sherry

2 tablespoons soy sauce
⅛ teaspoon cayenne
For Serving Day:
2 cups skim milk
¾ cup reduced-fat chicken
  broth
1½ cups couscous
cooking spray
fresh cilantro sprigs (optional)

ADVANCE PREP:

Place chicken between sheets of plastic wrap or wax paper. Pound with a meat mallet until ¼-inch thick. Cut chicken into ½-inch wide strips. Chop onion. Slice mushrooms.

PREPARATION:

In medium bowl, stir together cornstarch, ¼ cup broth, soy sauce, cayenne and sherry. In large skillet or saucepan, melt margarine over medium-high heat. Add onion and mushrooms; cook until onion is golden brown, stirring frequently; remove from heat. Remove onion mixture from skillet; set aside. Spray saucepan with cooking spray and place over medium-high heat; add chicken. Cook, stirring gently and frequently, until chicken is no longer pink. Add onion/mushroom mixture to cooked chicken; pour in cornstarch mixture and stir constantly over medium-high heat until sauce is thickened slightly and bubbly. Remove from heat. Cool. Place in labeled freezer bag; freeze.

TO SERVE:

Thaw chicken mixture. In large saucepan, stir together milk and remaining broth; heat to boiling. Stir in couscous, cover pan and remove from heat; let sit for 10 minutes until liquid is absorbed. Heat chicken mixture over medium heat in large skillet until heated through. Fluff couscous. Serve chicken beside couscous. Garnish with cilantro.

PER SERVING: 317.7 CALORIES; 3.4G FAT; 25.9G PROTEIN; 44.4G CARBOHYDRATES; 37MG CHOLESTEROL

Turkey Mini--Session

Roast Turkey Dinner
Turkey Potato Pie
Turkey Divan
Turkey Spaghetti Bake

Turkey Tetrazzini
Turkey-Asparagus Strata
Turkey Soup
Turkey Tortilla Casserole

Shopping List

MEAT
1 whole turkey (weight determined by chart on Roast Turkey page)

DAIRY
9 cups skim milk
4 eggs
butter
margarine
8-oz. fat-free cream cheese
4-oz. reduced-fat mozzarella cheese
2-oz. reduced-fat cheddar cheese
8-oz. low-fat Monterey Jack cheese
Parmesan cheese
sour cream

BREAD / PASTA
20-oz. dry spaghetti noodles
6-oz. elbow macaroni noodles
10 (6-inch) corn tortillas
10 slices bread, white or wheat

VEGETABLES
10 onions
1 large green bell pepper
9 celery ribs
8 large carrots
3 cups fresh mushrooms (sliced)
22 garlic cloves
1 bunch fresh parsley
1 cup asparagus (sliced)
2 bunches fresh spinach leaves
12 broccoli spears

CANNED / BOXED
48-oz. (6 cups) fat-free chicken broth—PLUS—1 cup (8-oz.) broth per pound of meat to freeze for turkey dinner
2 packets instant beef broth and seasoning mix
instant mashed potatoes
24-oz. tomato sauce
10-oz. can tomatoes and green chilies
7½-oz. can whole tomatoes

SPICES
basil
bay leaves
cilantro, dried
salt
black pepper
white pepper
sage
thyme
flour
paprika
parsley

FROZEN
2 cups frozen corn kernels

MISC.
2½ cups dry white wine
⅓ cup dry red wine
olive oil
vegetable oil
Dijon-style mustard

Preparation Instructions

TURKEY PREP:

1 whole turkey—prepare according to instructions in Roast Turkey recipe; cool completely; slice meat for roast turkey meat; remove remaining meat from bones; cube; reserve carcass for soup.

11 cups cooked turkey meat—cut into 1-inch cubes.

VEGETABLE PREP:

4 medium onions—cut into quarters.

6 medium onions—chop.

9 celery ribs—cut into 2-inch pieces

4 medium carrots—cut into 2-inch pieces

4 medium carrots—slice thinly.

1 large green bell pepper—chop.

14 garlic cloves—mince.

12 broccoli spears—steam until just tender; rinse in cold water; store covered in refrigerator until ready to use.

3 cups mushrooms—slice.

2 bunches fresh spinach leaves—tear into small pieces.

1 cup asparagus—slice thinly; in medium saucepan of boiling water, cook asparagus 3 minutes until just tender; drain; discard liquid; rinse under cold running water until cool; drain again.

1 bunch fresh parsley, chop

CHEESE PREP:

4-oz. (1 cup) reduced-fat mozzarella cheese—grate.

2-oz. (½ cup) reduced-fat cheddar cheese—grate.

8-oz. (2 cups) low-fat Monterey Jack cheese—grate.

ODDS AND ENDS PREP:

20-oz. dry spaghetti noodles—prepare according to package directions, cooking until just barely tender; drain and rinse in cold water; place cooked noodles in large bowl of cold water in refrigerator until ready to use.

Roast Turkey

You'll need a minimum 10-pound turkey for using in the turkey recipes. For the main roast turkey dinner, add ¾ pound per person to the 6 pounds already required for the other recipes.

Number of People = Weight of Turkey Needed to Buy

6 people =	14½ pounds
8 people =	16 pounds
10 people =	17½ pounds
12 people =	19 pounds
14 people =	20½ pounds
16 people =	22 pounds
18 people =	23½ pounds
20 people =	25 pounds

To Prepare Turkey:

3 onions, quartered

6 celery ribs, cut into two-inch pieces

2 medium carrots, cut into two-inch pieces

2 bay leaves

1½ cups dry white wine (or water)

1 tablespoon olive oil

2 teaspoons salt

2 teaspoons pepper

2 teaspoons sage

1 teaspoon thyme

fat-free canned chicken broth, 1 cup per pound (reserve until time to freeze meat)

Thaw turkey completely according to package directions. In bottom of deep roasting pan, place two quartered onions, four celery ribs, carrots, bay leaves and white wine (or water). Remove turkey giblets; rinse bird inside and out. Pat dry with paper towels. Stuff turkey loosely with remaining quartered onion and celery ribs. In small bowl, mix together olive oil, salt, pepper, sage and thyme. Brush turkey with olive oil mixture. Cover turkey loosely with a large sheet of foil coated lightly with olive oil, crimping foil on to edges of roasting pan. Cook according to chart below. During last 45 minutes of roasting time, cut band of skin or string between legs and tail. Uncover and continue roasting until done. Baste if desired.

TURKEY ROASTING CHART (LOOSELY WRAPPED WITH FOIL):
12 - 16 lbs / 325 degrees / 4 - 5 hours
16 - 20 lbs / 325 degrees / 5 - 6 hours
20 - 24 lbs / 325 degrees / 6 - 7 hours

Testing for Doneness:

About 20 minutes before roasting time is completed, test bird. Meat on thickest part of drumstick should feel soft when squeezed between fingers, drumstick should move up and down easily and meat thermometer inserted into thickest part of leg should read 185 degrees (or follow manufacturer's instructions).

FREEZING INSTRUCTIONS:
Pour liquid and drippings from roasting pan into a bowl. Remove vegetables. Allow to cool in refrigerator until fat congeals on top. Scoop off fat with a spoon and pour drippings into a labeled freezer bag. Thaw to use for making gravy on serving day.

Allow turkey to cool in pan for about 30 minutes; then place turkey and its roasting pan into refrigerator. Allow to cool completely (several hours). When fully chilled, slice turkey as usual. Remove all meat from bones. Place breast and dark meat slices into labeled freezer bags. Pour chicken broth into bags over meat. Freeze. Be sure to retain 12 cups of diced turkey meat for the other recipes.

TO SERVE:
Thaw bag of meat and broth and place into a covered baking dish for 30 minutes at 350 degrees. Or place turkey and broth into a microwave-safe dish covered dish, loosely cover and heat until hot (the time will vary with different microwaves, so check manufacturer's directions). Drain off broth (reserve to make more gravy, if needed). Arrange the heated turkey slices attractively on platter. Serve.

GRAVY INSTRUCTIONS:

2 tablespoons butter, margarine or
 ½ cup white wine
⅓ cup flour
½ teaspoon salt (optional)

3 cups thawed turkey drippings (if needed, add additional water, chicken broth or white wine to equal 3 cups)

In a medium saucepan, melt butter; thoroughly stir in flour and salt (if used). Heat over low to medium-low heat until bubbling, stirring constantly. Slowly pour liquid into flour and butter mixture, stirring constantly. Continue stirring and increase heat to medium. Continue stirring until gravy boils. Immediately reduce heat to low and simmer an additional two minutes, stirring frequently.

Turkey Potato Pie

6 servings

2 teaspoons vegetable oil
1½ cups onion, chopped
3 garlic cloves, minced
2 cups turkey meat, cooked and cubed
3 tablespoons flour
water

⅓ cup dry red table wine
2 packets instant beef broth and seasoning mix
3 tablespoons fresh parsley, chopped
1 cup instant mashed potatoes
1 tablespoon butter

ADVANCE PREP:

Cook and cube turkey meat. Chop onions. Mince garlic. Prepare potatoes; using fork, in medium bowl combine potato flakes, 2 cups boiling water, and the butter; mix until light and fluffy. Cool potatoes.

PREPARATION:

In large skillet heat oil; add onion and garlic and cook over high heat, stirring frequently, until onion begins to soften (about 1 minute). Remove from heat. Stir in turkey pieces. Sprinkle flour over turkey mixture and stir quickly to combine; return skillet to burner and cook over medium-high heat, stirring constantly, for 1 minute. Add ¾ cup water, red wine and broth mix; cook until mixture comes to a boil. Remove from heat; cool. Stir in parsley. Place turkey mixture and potatoes into separate labeled freezer bags; seal. Place both bags into an additional freezer bag; seal and freeze together.

TO SERVE:

Thaw both turkey and potato bags. Transfer turkey mixture into 2-quart casserole dish, top with potato mixture and spread over top of casserole. Bake at 350 for 20 - 30 minutes, or until turkey mixture is heated through and potato topping is golden brown.

PER SERVING: 297.8 CALORIES; 13.0G FAT; 18.9G PROTEIN; 25.2G CARBOHYDRATES; 53MG CHOLESTEROL.

Turkey Divan

6 servings

12 broccoli spears
3 tablespoons margarine
⅓ cup flour
½ teaspoon salt
¼ teaspoon white pepper
3 cups skim milk

8-oz. fat-free cream cheese, cut
  into small pieces
2 cups turkey meat, cooked and
  cubed
¼ teaspoon paprika
For Serving Day:
6 slices white bread, toasted

ADVANCE PREP:

Roast and cube turkey. Steam broccoli spears until just tender; cool.

PREPARATION:

In large skillet, melt margarine; sprinkle with flour, salt and pepper. Cook over
medium-high heat, stirring constantly, until mixture is bubbling (about 3
minutes). Gradually stir in milk; continuing to stir and cook until mixture is
thickened. Stir in cream cheese; cook, stirring constantly, until cheese is melted.
Stir in turkey pieces. Remove from heat; cool. Place turkey and cheese mixture
into a labeled freezer bag. Place steamed broccoli spears into a separate freezer
bag. Place both bags into a third freezer bag; seal and freeze.

TO SERVE:

Thaw both bags completely. Place sauce into saucepan; heat over low, stirring
constantly to recombine, until heated through. While sauce is heating, toast six
slices of white bread. Place toasted bread into bottom of 9x13-inch broiler-safe
pan. Divide broccoli spears and place on top of each piece of toast. Pour
turkey/cheese mixture over top of broccoli spears, dividing evenly. Sprinkle
lightly with paprika. Broil 4 inches from heat for about 1 minute, or until
cheese mixture is bubbling; remove from broiler. Serve.

PER SERVING: 314 CALORIES; 9.7G FAT; 32.1G PROTEIN; 29.4G CARBOHYDRATES; 48MG CHOLESTEROL.

Turkey Spaghetti Bake

6 servings

10-oz. spaghetti noodles, dry

2 tablespoons reduced-fat chicken broth

1½ cup green bell pepper, chopped

1 cup onion, chopped

6 garlic cloves, minced

2 cups turkey meat, cooked and cubed

½ teaspoon salt

½ teaspoon pepper

3 cups tomato sauce

1 tablespoon basil

⅓ cup fresh parsley, chopped

4-oz. (1 cup) reduced-fat mozzarella cheese, grated

ADVANCE PREP:

Roast and cube turkey. Prepare spaghetti noodles according to package directions until just barely tender; drain and rinse in cold water. Place cooked noodles in large bowl of cold water in refrigerator until ready to use. Chop green pepper and onion. Mince garlic. Grate mozzarella cheese.

PREPARATION:

In large skillet, heat chicken broth; add bell pepper, onion and garlic. Cook over medium-high heat, stirring frequently until vegetables are softened. Stir in turkey, salt, pepper and tomato sauce; bring mixture to a boil. Remove from heat; stir in basil and parsley. Spray 9x13-inch casserole dish with nonstick cooking spray. Spread half of cooked pasta evenly over bottom of casserole dish; top with half the turkey mixture. Repeat layers; sprinkle cheese evenly over top. Cover pan with foil; label and freeze.

TO SERVE:

Thaw. Preheat oven to 350 degrees. Bake, covered, 35 - 40 minutes, or until hot and bubbling. Garnish with fresh tomato slices and basil, if desired.

PER SERVING: 366.1 CALORIES; 4.8G FAT; 30.8G PROTEIN; 50.5G CARBOHYDRATES; 40MG CHOLESTEROL.

Turkey Tetrazzini

6 servings

10-oz. spaghetti noodles
2 tablespoons reduced-fat chicken broth
3 cups mushrooms, sliced
1 cup onion, chopped
¼ teaspoon thyme
½ teaspoon salt
½ teaspoon pepper
4 tablespoons flour

3 cups skim milk
1 cup canned fat-free chicken broth
½ cup dry white wine
2 cups turkey meat, cooked and cubed
¼ cup Parmesan cheese
3 tablespoons parsley

ADVANCE PREP:

Roast and cube turkey. Slice mushrooms. Chop onion. Prepare spaghetti noodles according to package directions until just barely tender; drain and rinse in cold water. Place cooked noodles in large bowl of cold water in refrigerator until ready to use.

PREPARATION:

In large skillet, heat 2 tablespoons chicken broth; add mushrooms, onion, thyme, salt and pepper. Cook over medium heat, stirring frequently, until mushrooms are golden brown (about 5 minutes). Stir flour, milk and broth into mushroom mixture; cook, until slightly thickened stirring constantly (about 1 minute). Remove from heat. Stir in wine. Place turkey and cooked spaghetti into large bowl; pour mushroom mixture over turkey and pasta; toss to combine. Spray 9x12-inch casserole dish with nonstick cooking spray. Transfer mixture to prepared dish; sprinkle with parsley and Parmesan cheese. Cool. Cover with foil; label and freeze.

TO SERVE:

Preheat oven to 375 degrees. Bake uncovered 25 - 35 minutes, or until lightly browned and bubbling.

PER SERVING: 395.8 CALORIES; 3.8G FAT; 34.9G PROTEIN; 53.8G CARBOHYDRATES; 37MG CHOLESTEROL.

Turkey-Asparagus Strata

8 servings

2 tablespoons reduced-fat
chicken broth
2 cups turkey meat, cooked and
cubed
3 garlic cloves, minced
1 medium onion, chopped
1 cup asparagus, sliced thinly
10 slices of bread (white or
wheat) crusts removed, cut
into 4 triangles each

3 cups skim milk
4 eggs
¼ cup flour
1 teaspoon Dijon mustard
½ teaspoon salt
¼ teaspoon pepper
2-oz. (½ cup) reduced-fat
cheddar cheese, grated

ADVANCE PREP:

Cook and cube turkey meat. Mince garlic. Chop onion. Slice asparagus. Grate
cheddar cheese. In medium saucepan of boiling water, cook asparagus 3
minutes, until just tender. Drain, discarding liquid; rinse under cold running
water until cool. Drain again.

PREPARATION:

In large skillet, heat chicken broth; add onion and garlic. Cook over medium
high heat, stirring frequently until onion is tender. Transfer cooked onion to
bowl; add cooked turkey and cooked asparagus; toss to combine. Spray 9x13-
inch baking dish with nonstick cooking spray. In bottom of baking dish, layer
bread triangles followed by turkey mixture. In separate medium-sized bowl, beat
together milk, eggs, flour, mustard, salt and pepper; pour over turkey and bread.
Sprinkle evenly with grated cheddar cheese. Cover pan with foil; label and
freeze.

TO SERVE:

Thaw. Preheat oven to 350 degrees. Bake 40 minutes, until mixture is set and
cheese is melted and lightly browned.

PER SERVING: 256.5 CALORIES; 5.5G FAT; 25.3G PROTEIN; 25.5G CARBOHYDRATES; 135MG CHOLESTEROL.

Turkey Soup

8 - 10 servings

1 turkey carcass, broken into pieces (left over from Roast Turkey Dinner)

4 cups canned fat-free chicken broth

10 cups water

2 whole carrots, cut into large chunks

3 medium celery ribs, cut into large chunks

1 onion, cut into four large pieces

8 garlic cloves, whole

3 bay leaves

4 carrots, sliced thinly

1 cup turkey meat, cooked and cubed

2 cups frozen corn kernels

1 teaspoon thyme

3 tablespoons parsley

6-oz. macaroni noodles

2 cups fresh spinach leaves, torn

ADVANCE PREP:

Roast turkey; reserve carcass. In large stockpot, place turkey carcass, chicken broth, water, large carrot chunks, celery, large onion pieces, whole garlic cloves and three bay leaves. Bring to boil; reduce heat to low and simmer for 1 ½ to 2 hours. Remove from heat and remove carcass and vegetables from broth.

PREPARATION:

Put stockpot of broth back onto burner. Stir in carrot slices, turkey meat, corn kernels, thyme and parsley. Heat to boiling; cook 5 minutes. Remove from heat; cool. Add noodles and spinach after soup cools. When soup has cooled pour into plastic freezer bag. Pour into large labeled freezer bag (use more than one bag if necessary).

TO SERVE:

Thaw. Pour into large stockpot. Heat over medium-high heat until heated through and noodles are tender.

PER SERVING: 180 CALORIES; 1.5G FAT; 17.1G PROTEIN; 29.4G CARBOHYDRATES; 10MG CHOLESTEROL.

Turkey Tortilla Casserole

6 servings

10 (6-inch) corn tortillas
vegetable oil
1 large onion, chopped
2 garlic cloves, minced
1 tablespoon vegetable oil
1 (10-oz.) can tomatoes and
green chilies, undrained and
chopped

Serving Day:
sour cream

1 (7 ½-oz) can whole tomatoes,
undrained and chopped
1 ½ teaspoons dried cilantro
¼ teaspoon salt
2 cups turkey meat, cooked and
cubed
8-oz. (2 cups) low-fat Monterey
Jack cheese, grated

ADVANCE PREP:

Roast and cube turkey. Grate cheese. Chop onion. Mince garlic.

PREPARATION:

Fry tortillas, one at a time, in ¼ inch hot oil about 5 seconds on each side or until softened. Drain on paper towels. Line an 11x6-inch baking dish with tortillas (tortillas can extend above top of pan, they'll shrink a bit when baked). Set aside. In large skillet heat 1 tablespoon oil; add onion and garlic; cook until tender. Stir in tomatoes, cilantro and salt. Simmer 5 minutes, stirring occasionally; stir in turkey. Pour turkey mixture over tortillas. Cool. Sprinkle with grated cheese. Cover with foil; label and freeze.

TO SERVE:

Thaw completely. Bake at 350 degrees for 25 - 30 minutes. Serve with sour cream, if desired.

PER SERVING: 318.1 CALORIES; 8.7G FAT; 31.8G PROTEIN; 26.5G CARBOHYDRATES; 46MG CHOLESTEROL.

Ground Turkey Mini-Session

Turkey Loaf
Turkey Burgers
Sloppy Turkey Joes
Turkey Lasagna Roll Ups

Shopping List

MEAT
5½ pounds lean ground turkey

DAIRY
4 eggs
1 cup fat-free cottage cheese
2-oz. reduced-fat mozzarella cheese
Parmesan cheese

BREAD / PASTA
rolled oats
3 slices bread (to make soft bread
    crumbs)
12 hamburger buns
11 large lasagna noodles

VEGETABLES
3 medium onions
2 red bell peppers
6 garlic cloves
1 bunch green onions
4-oz. fresh mushrooms

CANNED / BOXED
1 can fat-free chicken broth
8-oz. tomato sauce
26-oz. jar commercial spaghetti
    sauce

SPICES
oregano
salt
pepper
parsley
Italian seasoning

MISC.
⅓ cup dry bread crumbs
1 bottle chili sauce (or catsup)
dry white wine
cooking spray Worcestershire sauce
bottled hot red pepper sauce
red wine vinegar

Preparation Instructions

VEGETABLE PREP:

3 medium onions—chop finely.

¼ cup green onion—chop finely.

2 cups red bell pepper—chop.

4-oz. mushrooms—chop finely.

6 garlic cloves—mince.

CHEESE PREP:

2-oz. reduced-fat mozzarella cheese—grate.

MISC. PREP:

3 slices day old bread —remove crusts; crumble into crumbs.

Turkey Loaf

6 servings

2 pounds lean ground turkey
½ cups rolled oats
⅓ cup chili sauce (or catsup)
⅓ cup onion, chopped finely
1 egg

1 garlic clove, minced
1 teaspoon oregano
½ teaspoon salt
⅛ teaspoon pepper

ADVANCE PREP:
Chop onion. Mince garlic.

PREPARATION:
Preheat oven to 350 degrees. In a
large mixing bowl, combine all
turkey loaf ingredients. Mix well.
Make into loaf shape and place into
casserole dish. Bake 40 minutes.

Remove from oven and cool. Wrap, label and freeze.

TO SERVE:
Thaw. Bake at 325 degrees for 20 minutes or until heated through. Serve sliced
(also makes good meatloaf
sandwiches).

PER SERVING: 233.7 CALORIES; 12.6G FAT; 22.3G PROTEIN; 6.4G CARBOHYDRATES; 91MG CHOLESTEROL.

Turkey Burgers

6 servings

1 egg white
¼ cup dry white wine
⅓ cup soft bread crumbs
¼ teaspoon salt
⅛ teaspoon pepper
¼ cup green onions, chopped
   finely

1 pound lean ground turkey
4-oz. mushrooms, chopped
   finely
cooking spray
6 hamburger buns, split

ADVANCE PREP:

Make soft bread crumbs from 2 or 3 slices of day old bread. Chop green onions and mushrooms.

PREPARATION:

Beat egg white and wine until blended. Stir in bread crumbs, salt, pepper and green onions. Lightly mix in turkey and mushrooms. Shape mixture into 6 patties, each about ½ inch thick. Wrap individually in wax paper or clear plastic wrap; place patties into large labeled freezer bag; place bag of patties and bag of hamburger buns together into a second freezer bag; freeze together.

TO SERVE:

Thaw patties and buns completely. Place on broiler pan and broil about 6 inches from heat source, turning once, until patties are lightly browned on both sides and juices run clear when a knife is inserted in center (8 - 10 minutes). Serve hot in buns.

PER SERVING: 257.9 CALORIES; 8.6G FAT; 18.1 PROTEIN; 24.2G CARBOHYDRATES; 60MG CHOLESTEROL.

Sloppy Turkey Joes

6 servings

6 hamburger buns

2 teaspoons canned fat-free chicken broth

2 cups red bell peppers, chopped

1½ cups onion, chopped

4 cloves garlic, minced

¼ teaspoon black pepper

1½ pounds ground turkey

½ teaspoon salt (optional)

½ cup tomato sauce

¼ cup bottled chili sauce (or catsup)

1 tablespoon Worcestershire sauce

¼ teaspoon hot red pepper sauce (or to taste)

1 tablespoon red wine vinegar

ADVANCE PREP:

Chop red bell peppers and onions. Mince garlic.

PREPARATION:

Heat chicken broth in large skillet. Sauté bell peppers, onions, garlic and pepper over medium heat until vegetables are softened (3 minutes). Add turkey and salt. Stir to break up meat. Cook for 4 minutes or until meat is no longer pink. Stir in tomato sauce, chili sauce, Worcestershire sauce and hot red pepper sauce. Bring to a boil. Remove from heat. Stir in vinegar. Cool. Pour into labeled freezer bag. Place bag of meat and bag of hamburger buns together into a large freezer bag. Freeze together.

TO SERVE:

Thaw. Heat turkey mixture in skillet over medium heat until heated through. Serve in warmed buns.

PER SERVING: 330.0 CALORIES; 11.7G FAT; 24.9G PROTEIN; 30.6G CARBOHYDRATES; 90MG CHOLESTEROL.

Turkey Lasagna Roll Ups

8 servings

11 large lasagna noodles, uncooked
1 pound ground turkey
1 cup onion, chopped
1 garlic clove, minced
1 (26-oz.) jar commercial spaghetti sauce
¼ cup dry white wine
3 tablespoons parsley
½ teaspoon salt
1 cup fat-free cottage cheese
2-oz. (½ cup) reduced-fat mozzarella cheese, grated
2 eggs, slightly beaten
⅓ cup dry bread crumbs
1 teaspoon dried Italian seasoning
¼ cup Parmesan cheese

ADVANCE PREP:

Chop onion. Mince garlic. Grate cheese. Cook lasagna noodles according to package directions; drain and rinse in cold water. Carefully cut in half crosswise to make two long thin triangles from each noodle. Store in large pan full of cold water in refrigerator until ready to use.

PREPARATION:

Cook turkey, onion and garlic in large skillet until turkey is browned, stirring to crumble meat. Add spaghetti sauce, wine, parsley and salt. Stir well and cover. Simmer 10 minutes, stirring occasionally. Remove from heat and set aside. Combine cottage cheese and next 4 ingredients, stirring well. Spread mixture evenly over lasagna noodles. Roll up jelly roll fashion, starting at narrow end. Place lasagna rolls, seam side down in a lightly greased 13x9x2-inch baking dish. Pour meat sauce over rolls and sprinkle with Parmesan cheese. Cover pan with foil; label and freeze.

TO SERVE:

Thaw. Bake, covered, at 375 degrees for 30 minutes. Uncover and bake for 15 minutes or until heated through.

PER SERVING: 462.5 CALORIES; 13.7G FAT; 24.8G PROTEIN; 58.7G CARBOHYDRATES; 80MG CHOLESTEROL.

Ground Beef
Mini-Session

Meatballs and Sauce
Beef Loaf
Pizza Burgers
Macaroni and Beef
Tortilla Casserole

Shopping List

MEAT
6 pounds extra-lean ground beef

DAIRY
1 cup skim milk
12-oz. fat-free mozzarella cheese
¾ cup non-fat sour cream
Parmesan cheese
2 eggs
butter

BREAD / PASTA
1 cup dry bread crumbs
5 slices bread for soft crumbs
6-oz. elbow macaroni, dry
6 corn tortillas
6 hamburger buns

VEGETABLES
3 medium onions
1 pound carrots
1 medium red bell pepper
3 medium zucchini
2 garlic cloves

½ cup mushrooms, sliced
1 bunch fresh cilantro

CANNED / BOXED
1 package taco seasoning mix
1 (24-oz.) can tomato sauce
1 (32-oz.) can crushed tomatoes
1 (14.5-oz.) can diced tomatoes
1 (16-oz.) can red kidney beans
1 (4.5-oz.) can chopped green
  chilies

SPICES
basil
oregano
thyme
sage
parsley
salt
pepper

MISC.
apple juice (or white wine)

Preparation Instructions

VEGETABLE PREP:

3 medium zucchinis—grate.

3 medium onions—chop.

1 medium red bell pepper —chop.

1 pound carrots—shred.

2 garlic cloves—mince.

½ cup mushrooms—slice thinly.

CHEESE PREP:

12-oz. fat-free mozzarella cheese—grate.

MISC. PREP:

6-oz. elbow macaroni—cook according to package directions; drain and rinse in cold water; store in large pan full of cold water in refrigerator until ready to use.

3 slices day old bread—remove crust; cut or crumble into crumbs.

Meatballs and Sauce

6 servings

1 cup dry bread crumbs
¾ cup skim milk
2 pounds extra lean ground
   beef
1½ cup grated zucchini
¾ cup apple juice (or white
   wine)

3 tablespoons Parmesan cheese
3 tablespoons tomato paste
1 tablespoon oregano
32-oz. canned crushed tomatoes
1 cup water

ADVANCE PREP:

Grate zucchini.

PREPARATION:

Mix bread crumbs and milk. Let stand 5 minutes. Add beef, zucchini, 2
tablespoons apple juice, cheese, tomato paste and 1 teaspoon oregano. Mix well.
Form into 36 equal meatballs. Spray large skillet with nonstick cooking spray;
heat. Add meatballs, cook over medium-high heat turning as needed, until
browned on all sides (about 10 minutes). Remove meatballs from skillet; set
aside. In same skillet, cook remaining apple juice over medium-high heat,
scraping brown bits from bottom of skillet. Add tomatoes, remaining oregano
and water. Reduce heat to low; add meatballs. Simmer, covered, 30-40 minutes
until meatballs are cooked through. Place into labeled freezer bag; freeze.

TO SERVE:

Thaw. Heat in skillet over medium heat until heated through.

PER SERVING: 270.8 CALORIES; 11.5G FAT; 15.8G PROTEIN; 26.8G CARBOHYDRATES; 40MG CHOLESTEROL.

Beef Loaf

8 servings

2 cups onion, chopped
2 cups carrots, shredded
2 cups zucchini, shredded
2 garlic cloves, minced
1 cup fresh bread crumbs
4 tablespoons skim milk
1 pound extra-lean ground beef

2 eggs, slightly beaten
2 tablespoons parsley
½ teaspoon salt
2 teaspoons pepper
1 teaspoon thyme
½ teaspoon sage

ADVANCE PREP:

Chop onions. Shred carrots and zucchini. Mince garlic. Prepare soft bread crumbs.

PREPARATION:

Spray medium skillet with cooking spray. Heat and add onions. Cook over medium-high heat, stirring frequently until golden brown. Add carrot, zucchini and garlic, stirring constantly until vegetables are softened. Remove from heat. Set aside. In small bowl, combine bread crumbs and milk. Let stand five minutes. In large bowl, combine beef, eggs, parsley, salt, pepper, thyme, sage, cooled vegetables and soaked bread crumbs. Shape into loaf. Place into center of 13x9x2-inch baking dish. Bake 1 hour and 15 minutes. Remove from oven. Cool. Wrap, label and freeze.

TO SERVE:

Either thaw and reheat in microwave or thaw and bake at 350 degrees for 30 minutes or until heated through.

PER SERVING: 206.4 CALORIES; 10.3G FAT; 13.7G PROTEIN; 15.1G CARBOHYDRATES; 105MG CHOLESTEROL.

Pizza Burgers

6 servings

1 pound extra-lean ground beef
1 teaspoon salt
1 teaspoon pepper
1 teaspoon oregano
½ cup tomato sauce
½ cup mushrooms, thinly
  sliced

1 tablespoon butter
4-oz. (1 cup) fat-free mozzarella
  cheese, grated
1 tablespoon parsley
6 hamburger buns

ADVANCE PREP:
Slice mushrooms. Grate cheese.

PREPARATION:
In skillet over medium-high heat, sauté mushroom slices in butter. Remove
from heat. Cool. Place mushroom slices into small, labeled freezer bag. In large
bowl combine beef, salt, pepper and oregano. Form beef mixture into six equal
patties; wrap individually; place into labeled freezer bag. Place mushroom bag
and beef patties bag into an additional labeled freezer bag. Freeze together.

TO SERVE:
Thaw, cook patties in nonstick skillet for 3 minutes. Spread each patty with 1
tablespoon tomato sauce
and 1 tablespoon mushrooms. Divide cheese evenly between patties. Cook,
covered, until patties are cooked through and cheese is melted. Serve sprinkled
with parsley in hamburger buns.
PER SERVING: 217.1 CALORIES; 13.1G FAT; 21.0G PROTEIN; 3.5G CARBOHYDRATES; 56MG CHOLESTEROL.

Macaroni and Beef

6 servings

6-oz. elbow macaroni
1 pound extra-lean ground beef
1 cup onion, chopped
1 cup red bell pepper, chopped
1 cup tomato sauce

½ teaspoon dried basil
½ teaspoon thyme
¼ teaspoon pepper
4-oz. (1 cup) reduced-fat
    mozzarella cheese, grated

ADVANCE PREP:

Grate cheese. Chop onion and red bell pepper. Cook macaroni according to package directions; drain and rinse in cold water; place into large pan full of cold water in refrigerator until ready to use.

PREPARATION:

In large skillet, brown ground beef, onion and bell pepper until meat is no longer pink and vegetables are softened. Add tomato sauce, basil, thyme and pepper. Stir frequently over medium heat until heated through. Remove from heat. Add macaroni; stir to combine. Cool. Freeze in labeled freezer bag. Place grated mozzarella cheese in freezer bag and attach to macaroni mixture bag.

TO SERVE:

Thaw completely. Place in 1-quart baking dish. Sprinkle evenly with cheese. Bake 20-30 minutes until bubbling and lightly browned.

PER SERVING: 292.2 CALORIES; 10.3G FAT; 21.3G PROTEIN; 28.3G CARBOHYDRATES; 43MG CHOLESTEROL.

Tortilla Casserole

6 servings

1 pound extra-lean ground beef
1 (15-oz.) can red kidney beans, drained and rinsed
1 (14.5-oz.) can diced tomatoes, undrained
1 (4.5-oz.) can chopped green chilies

1 package taco seasoning mix
6 corn tortillas
¾ cup nonfat sour cream
4 oz. (1 cup) mozzarella or cheddar cheese, grated
2 tablespoons chopped fresh cilantro

ADVANCE PREP:

Chop cilantro. Grate cheese.

ADVANCE:

Spray nonstick skillet with nonstick cooking spray. Heat over high heat until hot. Add ground beef; brown 8 - 10 minutes or until thoroughly cooked, stirring constantly. Drain well; return beef to skillet. Add beans, tomatoes, chilies and taco seasoning mix; mix well. Reduce heat; simmer 5 minutes.

Meanwhile, spray 12x8 (2-quart) baking dish with nonstick cooking spray. Cut each tortilla in half; place 6 halves in bottom of sprayed baking dish, overlapping slightly. Spoon half of beef mixture evenly over tortillas. Spoon sour cream over beef

mixture; spread evenly. Top with remaining 6 tortilla halves and remaining beef mixture. Cover tightly with foil; label and freeze.

TO SERVE:

Thaw. Bake at 350 degrees for 45 minutes. Remove from oven; sprinkle with cheese. Cover; let stand 3 minutes or until cheese is melted. Sprinkle with cilantro. Serve hot.

PER SERVING: 324.9 CALORIES; 10.8G FAT; 23.8G PROTEIN; 34.2G CARBOHYDRATES; 45MG CHOLESTEROL.

Beef Mini-Session

Country Beef Soup
Old-Fashioned Beef Stew
Braised Beef
Beef Fajitas
Beef and Noodles

Shopping List

MEAT
6 pounds lean boneless beef

DAIRY
8-oz. reduced-fat cheddar cheese
margarine
fat-free sour cream

BREAD / PASTA
12 flour tortillas
6-oz. wide egg noodles

VEGETABLES
10 medium onions
1 pound potatoes
1 pound small red potatoes
3 large ribs celery
1 green bell pepper
1½ cups baby carrots
4½ cups mushrooms
1½ pounds carrots
3 garlic cloves
1½ cups pearl onions
1 head lettuce

CANNED / BOXED
2 cans Italian-style stewed tomatoes

36-oz. (4½ cups) canned fat-free
   beef broth
6 packets instant beef broth and
   seasoning mix
small can tomato paste

SPICES
parsley
salt
pepper
flour
thyme
tarragon
bay leaves
oregano
cumin
paprika

FROZEN
1 cup frozen whole kernel corn

MISC.
olive oil
dry red wine
lime juice
1 cup salsa
prepared mustard
red-wine vinegar

Preparation Instructions

MEAT PREP:

2 pounds beef—cut into 2-inch cubes.

2 pounds beef—cut into ¼-inch strips.

VEGETABLE PREP:

5½ cups onion—chop.

3 medium onions—slice thinly.

1 green bell pepper—slice.

4 cups carrots—chop.

3 garlic cloves—mince.

1 pound small red potatoes—cut into quarters; store in large pan of water in refrigerator until ready to use.

1 pound regular potatoes—peel and cut into ½-inch cubes.

1 lime—squeeze juice into small bowl.

3 cups mushrooms—remove ends.

Country Beef Soup

6 servings

6 cups water

3 cups canned Italian-style stewed tomatoes (cut up and reserve liquid)

1 pound potatoes, peeled and cut into ½-inch cubes

1 pound cooked beef, diced

1½ cups celery, sliced

1½ cups mushrooms, sliced

1½ cups carrots, sliced

1 cup onion, chopped

1 cup frozen whole-kernel corn

6 packets instant beef broth and seasoning mix

2 tablespoons parsley

1 teaspoon pepper

ADVANCE PREPARATION:

Dice beef; sauté in large skillet until cooked through. Peel potatoes; cut into ½-inch cubes; store in large pan of cold water in refrigerator until ready to use. Slice celery, mushrooms and carrots. Chop onion.

PREPARATION:

Combine all ingredients in large stockpot or Dutch oven. Heat to a boil and cook until potatoes are not quite tender. Remove from heat and cool quickly. Pour into labeled freezer bags. Freeze.

TO SERVE:

Thaw; heat in Dutch oven over medium-high heat until heated through.

PER SERVING: 329.0 CALORIES; 15.5G FAT; 19.3G PROTEIN; 30.9G CARBOHYDRATES; 51MG CHOLESTEROL.

Old-Fashioned Beef Stew

6 servings

1 tablespoon olive oil
1½ cups onion, chopped
2 garlic cloves, minced
3 teaspoons flour
1 teaspoon salt
½ teaspoon pepper
1 pound lean boneless beef, cut
  into 2-inch cubes
1 pound small red potatoes,
  quartered

1 cup small white mushrooms,
  ends removed
1½ cup pearl onions
1½ cup baby carrots
3 cups reduced-fat beef broth
½ cup red wine vinegar
2 tablespoons tomato paste
½ teaspoon thyme
½ teaspoon tarragon
2 bay leaves
2 tablespoons parsley

ADVANCE PREP:

Chop onions. Mince garlic. Cut beef into 2-inch cubes. Cut small red potatoes into quarters; store in large pan of water in refrigerator until ready to use.

PREPARATION:

In large skillet, cook onions and garlic in olive oil until softened. On a plate, combine flour, half the salt, half the pepper. Dredge beef with flour mixture to coat evenly. Add beef to onion mixture, cook stirring frequently until beef is browned on all sides. Add mushrooms, pearl onions and carrots; cook stirring frequently 2 minutes. Add broth, vinegar, tomato paste, thyme, tarragon, bay leaves, remaining salt and pepper, and 5 cups water. Bring to boil. Reduce heat to low and simmer covered 20 minutes. Add potatoes. Cook an additional 5 minutes (potatoes will still be firm). Remove from heat. Cool quickly. Freeze in labeled freezer bags.

TO SERVE:

Thaw. Heat over medium heat until heated through. Discard bay leaves, stir in parsley. Serve hot.

PER SERVING: 303.7 CALORIES; 12.8G FAT; 24.8G PROTEIN; 28.3G CARBOHYDRATES; 48MG CHOLESTEROL.

Braised Beef

6 servings

1 tablespoon olive oil	¼ teaspoon salt
4 cups onion, chopped	1 cup dry red wine
4 cups carrots, chopped	1 bay leaf
1 garlic clove, minced	1 teaspoon oregano
2 pounds lean boneless beef	1 teaspoon thyme

ADVANCE PREP:

Chop onion and carrots. Mince garlic.

PREPARATION:

In Dutch oven, heat oil, add onions. Cook over medium-high heat stirring frequently until onions are golden brown. Add carrots and garlic. Cook until carrots are tender. Add beef to vegetable mixture; stir frequently and cook until beef is browned. Stir in remaining ingredients; bring to boil. Reduce heat and simmer, covered, for 1½ hours (add small amounts of water as needed to keep meat from sticking to pan). Remove beef from pan; slice. Cool. Place meat and vegetable mixture into labeled freezer bags. Freeze.

TO SERVE:

Thaw. Reheat in large skillet. Serve hot.

PER SERVING: 438.2 CALORIES; 23.0G FAT; 32.8G PROTEIN; 18.0G CARBOHYDRATES; 97MG CHOLESTEROL.

Beef Fajitas

6 servings

1 pound lean boneless beef, cut into ¼-inch strips	¼ cup lime juice
1 teaspoon cumin	*For Serving Day:*
1 teaspoon chili powder	12 (6-inch) flour tortillas
½ teaspoon pepper	2 cups shredded lettuce
1 green bell pepper, seeded and sliced	8-oz. (2 cups) reduced-fat cheddar cheese, grated
1 cup onion, sliced	1 cup salsa

ADVANCE PREP:

Slice onion and green pepper. Cut raw meat into ¼-inch slices. Store in refrigerator until ready to use.

PREPARATION:

Sprinkle beef on all sides with cumin, chili powder and black pepper. Spray large skillet with cooking spray. Heat. Add bell pepper and onion; cook over high heat stirring constantly until vegetables are lightly browned. Add beef, stirring constantly until beef is no longer pink. Add lime juice; toss to combine. Cool. Put into labeled freezer bag. Freeze.

TO SERVE:

Thaw completely. Reheat meat mixture in large skillet until heated through. Warm tortillas in microwave if desired. To assemble fajitas, place an equal amount of beef mixture onto center of each tortilla, top beef with ¼ cup lettuce, an equal amount of cheese and 2 tablespoons salsa. Roll tortillas to enclose filling.

PER SERVING: 386.0 CALORIES; 7.8G FAT; 31.8G PROTEIN; 47.3G CARBOHYDRATES; 41MG CHOLESTEROL.

Beef and Noodles

6 servings

1 pound lean boneless beef, cut into ¼-inch strips

2 medium onions, thinly sliced

2 cups small mushrooms, ends removed

2 tablespoons margarine

2 tablespoons flour

1 ½ cup fat-free beef broth

1 teaspoon prepared mustard

½ teaspoon paprika

½ teaspoon salt

¼ teaspoon pepper

¼ cup fat-free sour cream

6-oz. wide egg noodles (for serving day)

ADVANCED PREP:

Cut beef into ½-inch strips. Slice onions. Store in refrigerator until ready to use.

PREPARATION:

Spray large skillet with cooking spray. Cook beef over medium-high heat until no longer pink, stirring frequently. Remove from skillet. In same skillet, add onions, cooking until golden brown. Add mushrooms, cooking until softened and lightly browned. Remove vegetables from skillet. In same skillet, melt margarine, sprinkle with flour. Cook over medium-high heat until bubbling, stirring constantly. While continuing to stir, add broth, mustard, paprika, salt and pepper. Cook, stirring constantly, until mixture is thickened. Remove from heat. Stir in sour cream. Return beef, onions and mushrooms to skillet and stir gently to coat. Pour into labeled freezer bags. Freeze.

TO SERVE:

Thaw completely. Warm meat mixture until heated through. Cook noodles. Serve beef over hot cooked noodles.

PER SERVING: 322.6 CALORIES; 11.4G FAT; 25.9G PROTEIN; 32.0G CARBOHYDRATES; 76MG CHOLESTEROL.

Pork Chop Mini-Session

Dijon Pork Chops
Sweet-n-Sour Pork
Pork Rice Skillet Bake
Herbed Pork Chops
Provencale Pork
Stuffed Pork Chops

Shopping List

MEAT
18 regular pork chops
6 thick-cut pork chops (about 1-inch thick; ask your butcher)
3½ pounds boneless pork chops

DAIRY
Parmesan cheese
1 egg
butter
margarine

BREAD / PASTA
½ cup dry bread crumbs
1 box wild rice mix

VEGETABLES
4 medium onions
1 large green bell pepper
3 garlic cloves
2 large tomatoes
2 cups mushrooms, sliced
1½ pounds potatoes
1 bunch fresh parsley

CANNED / BOXED
1 (15-oz.) can stewed tomatoes

2 cups canned pineapple chunks
1½ cups fat-free beef broth
1 package brown and wild rice mushroom recipe mix

SPICES
basil
cayenne
parsley
paprika
mixed herbs
fennel
marjoram
salt
pepper
cornstarch
sugar

MISC.
vegetable oil
Dijon-style mustard
white vinegar
catsup
soy sauce
⅓ cup cooking sherry
⅓ cup dry white wine

Preparation

MEAT PREPARATION:

1½ pounds pork chops—trim off any fat and cut into 1-inch pieces.

2 pounds pork chops—cut into ½-inch strips.

VEGETABLE PREPARATION:

1 large onion—cut into thin wedges.

3 medium onions—slice thinly.

1 medium onion—chop.

1 large green pepper—cut into 1-inch squares.

1½ pounds potatoes—peel and slice thinly; store in large bowl filled with water in refrigerator until ready to use.

3 garlic cloves—mince.

1 large tomato—cut into wedges.

1 large tomato—slice.

½ cup fresh parsley—chop.

2 cups mushrooms—slice.

MISC. PREPARATION:

Wild rice mix—cook according to package directions substituting ⅓ cup sherry for ⅓ cup water.

Dijon Pork Chops

6 servings

½ cup plain dried bread crumbs
3 tablespoons Parmesan cheese
3 tablespoons parsley
1 tablespoon vegetable oil

½ teaspoon pepper
6 pork chops
2 tablespoons Dijon mustard

ADVANCE PREP:

None.

PREPARATION:

In pie plate, combine bread crumbs, Parmesan cheese, parsley, oil and pepper. Mix well. Set aside. Spread both sides of pork chops with mustard; press chops into bread crumb mixture, coating both sides. Spray rack in broiler pan with cooking spray, arrange chops on rack; broil 5 to 6 inches from element until cooked (5 - 6 minutes on each side). Remove from heat. Cool. Place chops in single layer onto cookie sheet; freeze. As soon as chops are frozen solid, remove from  baking sheet and place frozen chops together in labeled freezer bag; return to freezer.

TO SERVE:

Thaw. Reheat chops in skillet over medium heat until heated through, turning once.

PER SERVING: 297.6 CALORIES; 13.3G FAT; 35.5G PROTEIN; 7.5G CARBOHYDRATES; 81MG CHOLESTEROL.

Sweet-n-Sour Pork

6 servings

¾ cup cornstarch
⅓ cup white vinegar
⅓ cup sugar
1 cup water
2 tablespoons catsup
1½ tablespoons soy sauce
⅛ teaspoon cayenne
1 egg, beaten
6 boneless pork chops, trimmed and cut into 1-inch chunks

1 large onion, cut into thin wedges
1 large green pepper, seeded and cut into 1-inch squares
2 garlic cloves, minced
1 large tomato, cut into wedges
2 cups canned pineapple chunks, drained
1 cup water

ADVANCE PREP:

Trim pork chops and cut into 1-inch pieces. Cut onion into thin wedges. Cut green pepper into 1-inch squares. Mince garlic. Cut tomato into wedges.

PREPARATION:

For sweet-and-sour sauce: in a medium sized bowl, combine ¼ cup cornstarch and the vinegar. Stir in 1 cup water, sugar, catsup, soy sauce and cayenne; set aside. In small bowl, beat egg. In separate bowl, place remaining cornstarch. Dip pork chunks in egg; then dip into cornstarch. Over medium-high heat, heat vegetable oil in large skillet. Add meat to hot oil and sauté until golden brown on the outside and no longer pink inside (stirring constantly); remove meat from pan (use slotted spoon). Add onion, green pepper, garlic and 2 tablespoons water to pan; sauté for 1 minute. Stir sweet-and-sour sauce into pan with vegetables. Cook stirring constantly until sauce boils and thickens. Remove from heat. Add tomato and pineapple. Freeze sauce and meat chunks separately; attach bags together.

TO SERVE:

Thaw. Heat sauce and meat in separate skillets over medium-high heat. Pour sauce over meat to serve.

PER SERVING: 262.3 CALORIES; 4.2G FAT; 26.3G PROTEIN; 30.7G CARBOHYDRATES; 74MG CHOLESTEROL.

Pork Rice Skillet Bake

6 servings

6 pork chops
1 package brown and wild rice
    mushroom mix
2 cups water

1 large tomato, sliced
1 large onion, sliced
½ cup fresh parsley, chopped

ADVANCE PREP:

Slice onion and tomato. Chop fresh parsley.

PREPARATION:

Spray large nonstick skillet with nonstick cooking spray. Heat over high heat; place chops in skillet; cook 2 minutes, turning halfway through. Remove from heat. Remove pork chops from skillet; set aside. In freeze-able casserole dish, stir together drippings from browning pork chops, the wild rice mix (and seasoning packet) and 2 cups water. Arrange slices of tomato and onion in a single layer over rice mixture. Sprinkle with ½ cup parsley. Arrange pork chops over top. Cover. Bake in 350 degree oven for 30 minutes, or until pork is no longer pink in center. Cool in refrigerator until room temperature. Cover; label and freeze.

TO SERVE:

Thaw. Bake in 350 degree oven for 20 minutes or until heated through. Serve hot.

PER SERVING: 411.9 CALORIES; 19.4G FAT; 34.5G PROTEIN; 24.2G CARBOHYDRATES; 95MG CHOLESTEROL.

Herbed Pork Chops

6 servings

⅓ cup dry white wine
2 teaspoons fennel, crushed
1 teaspoon marjoram
¼ teaspoon salt

1 garlic clove, minced
6 pork chops
2 teaspoons basil

ADVANCE PREP:

Mince garlic.

PREPARATION:

Combine together in small bowl: wine, fennel, marjoram, basil, salt and garlic; blend well. Set aside. Spray large skillet with cooking spray. Cook pork chops over medium-high heat for 3 minutes. Turn chops, add wine mixture. Reduce heat; cover and simmer for 5 minutes or until pork is no longer pink. Remove from heat. Cool. Place chops with wine sauce into labeled freezer bags. Freeze.

TO SERVE:

Thaw. Place chops with wine mixture into large skillet; reheat until heated through. Serve with wine sauce poured over the top of the pork chops.

PER SERVING: 310.6 CALORIES; 18.9G FAT; 29.9G PROTEIN; 1.2G CARBOHYDRATES; 95MG CHOLESTEROL.

Provencale Pork

6 servings

2 pounds boneless pork chops,
  cut into ½-inch strips
¼ cup butter
2 medium onions, sliced
1 (15-oz.) can stewed tomatoes
½ teaspoon salt

¼ teaspoon pepper
½ teaspoon dried mixed herbs
1½ pounds potatoes, peeled
  and thinly sliced
1 tablespoon chopped parsley
  (for garnish)

ADVANCE PREP:

Trim any excess fat off pork chops; slice into thin strips. Slice onions. Peel potatoes; slice thinly; store in large bowl filled with water in refrigerator until ready to use.

PREPARATION:

In large skillet over medium heat, melt half the butter. Add slices of pork; cook, stirring constantly, until no longer pink. Remove meat from skillet; set aside. Stir onions into juices remaining in pan; cook until just tender. Add tomatoes, salt, pepper and mixed herbs to pan. Heat to boil; reduce heat; simmer about 5 minutes. In a freeze-able casserole dish, layer pork, sauce and potatoes (end with potato layer). Brush top of potatoes with melted butter; sprinkle with parsley. Cover casserole dish with a lid and bake at 350 degrees for 1 hour. Remove from oven; cool. Label and freeze.

TO SERVE:

Thaw. Bake, uncovered, for 1 hour at 350 degrees.

PER SERVING: 323.9 CALORIES; 15.0G FAT; 26.3G PROTEIN; 20.4G CARBOHYDRATES; 74MG CHOLESTEROL.

Stuffed Pork Chops

6 servings

6 thick-cut pork chops (about 1-inch thick; ask your butcher)
½ cup wild rice mix
2 tablespoons margarine or butter
2 cups mushrooms, sliced

⅓ cup sherry
½ cup onion, chopped
2 teaspoons pepper
1½ teaspoons paprika
1½ cups fat-free beef broth
2 tablespoons cornstarch

ADVANCE PREP:

Chop onion. Slice mushrooms. Cook wild rice mixture according to package directions, substituting • cup sherry for • cup water in directions.

PREPARATION:

Heat butter in skillet; stir in mushroom slices and onions, cook until softened. Remove from heat. Stir ½ mushrooms into wild rice mixture. Slice a pocket in each chop. Spoon 2 - 3 tablespoons wild rice mixture into each chop. Close with toothpicks. Rub pepper and paprika into chops. Broil chops on broiler rack 5-inches from the heat for 15 minutes (turning halfway through). Cool slightly. Remove toothpicks. For sauce, in saucepan stir together broth and cornstarch. Add remaining sautéed mushrooms; cook and stir until thickened and bubbly. Cook and stir for 2 minutes more. Stir in 1 tablespoon sherry. Place chops and sauce in large freezer bag; label and freeze.

TO SERVE:

Thaw. Place in 13x9x2-inch casserole dish. Bake at 375 for 1 hour or until heated through. Spoon sauce over chops before serving.

PER SERVING: 397.8 CALORIES; 19.3G FAT; 35.6G PROTEIN; 17.5G CARBOHYDRATES; 95MG CHOLESTEROL.

Crab Mini-Session

Crab Quesadillas
Crab Rice Chowder
Crab-stuffed Manicotti

Crab Quiche
Crab Strata

Shopping List

MEAT
5 (7.5-oz.) cans crab meat

DAIRY
3-oz. reduced-fat Monterey Jack
cheese
4-oz. reduced-fat cheddar cheese
4-oz. reduced-fat Swiss cheese
10 eggs (or equivalent egg
substitute)
1½ cups 2% milk (or fat-free
evaporated canned milk)
5½ cups skim milk
1½ cups fat-free cottage cheese
margarine
Parmesan cheese

BREAD / PASTA
12 flour tortillas
8 slices bread (wheat or white)
6 manicotti shells

VEGETABLES
4 garlic cloves
2 bunches green onions
1 medium onion
1 cup mushrooms, sliced
2 cups broccoli florette's
1 small red bell pepper
2 ribs celery
1 bunch fresh cilantro

CANNED / BOXED
4-oz can green
chilies
2¼ cups fat-free
chicken broth
long grain white
rice
1 (17-oz.) can cream-style corn

SPICES
cilantro
honey
soy sauce
salt
pepper
lemon peel
dry mustard
nutmeg or ground mace
⅛ cup sliced almonds
thyme
onion powder
Italian spice mix

MISC.
dry white wine
lemon juice
vegetable oil
Dijon-style mustard
bottled hot pepper sauce
flour
prepared mustard

Preparation Instructions

CHEESE PREP:

3-oz. (¾ cup) reduced-fat Monterey Jack cheese—grate.

4-oz. (1 cup) Swiss cheese—grate.

4-oz. (1 cup) reduced-fat cheddar cheese—grate.

VEGETABLE PREP:

1 bunch green onions—slice.

1 cup onion—chop.

¼ cup celery—slice thinly.

1 cup mushrooms—slice.

2 cups broccoli florettes—chop coarsely.

½ cup red bell pepper—chop finely.

1 bunch fresh cilantro—chop.

4 garlic cloves—mince.

Crab Quesadillas

6 servings

1 (4-oz.) can green chilies
¼ cup dry white wine
1 tablespoon lemon juice
1 cup fresh cilantro, chopped
¼ cup reduced-fat chicken
  broth
1 tablespoon honey

1 (7.5-oz.) can crab meat,
  drained and flaked
3-oz. (¾ cup) reduced-fat
  Monterey Jack cheese, grated
1 cup sliced green onions
12 flour tortillas

ADVANCED PREP:

Grate Monterey Jack cheese. Slice green onions.

PREPARATION:

In blender, blend chilies, wine and lemon juice until smooth. Pour into a 2-quart saucepan. Bring to boil; continue to boil, stirring frequently until reduced to · cup. Return mixture to blender. Add cilantro leaves, chicken broth and honey. Blend to combine. Place sauce in small labeled freezer bag. In mixing bowl, combine crab, cheese and sliced onions. Place into labeled freezer bag. In large freezer bag, put the bag of chili sauce, the bag of crab mixture and the bag of tortillas. Seal and freeze.

TO SERVE:

Thaw. Spray two cookie sheets with cooking spray. Place 6 tortillas in a single layer onto cookie sheets. Divide crab mixture evenly between tortillas. Spread almost to edge of tortilla. Top each tortilla with remaining tortillas. On two oven racks, bake in 450 degree oven until tortillas are lightly browned (halfway through baking time, switch cookie sheets in the oven). Slide quesadillas onto cutting board; cut each into 6 wedges. Serve with cold chili sauce.

Variation: 2 medium tomatoes can be seeded, diced and sprinkled on top of crab mixture before adding second tortillas.

PER SERVING: 421.7 CALORIES; 9.1G FAT; 26.2 PROTEIN; 58.2G CARBOHYDRATES; 42MG CHOLESTEROL.

Crab Quiche

6 servings

CRUST:
1 cup rice, cooked (white or
   brown)

FILLING:
4-oz. (1 cup) Swiss cheese,
   grated
1 (7½-oz.) can crab meat,
   drained and flaked
2 green onions, sliced
4 eggs, beaten

1 egg, beaten
teaspoon soy sauce

1½ cups 2% milk (or fat-free
   evaporated milk)
½ teaspoon salt (optional)
½ teaspoon lemon peel, grated
¼ teaspoon dry mustard
dash nutmeg or ground mace
⅛ cup sliced almonds

ADVANCE PREP:
Cook rice (or use leftover rice for crust). Grate Swiss cheese. Slice green onions.

PREPARATION:
Crust: Mix together cooked rice, egg and soy sauce. Spray 9-inch pie plate with
cooking spray. Spread rice mixture evenly to cover pie plate. Bake rice crust at
350 degrees for 10 minutes. Remove from oven.

   Filling: Arrange grated cheese on bottom of pie crust. Top with crab meat.
Sprinkle with green onions. Mix together eggs, milk, salt, lemon peel, mustard
and nutmeg. Pour evenly over top of quiche. Sprinkle almonds over top. Bake at
350 degrees for 45 minutes, or until set. Remove from oven and let sit 10
minutes before slicing, if serving fresh; or wrap pie pan, label and freeze.

TO SERVE:
Thaw. Can be served cold for a hot weather meal. Or heat thawed quiche in
350 degree oven for 20 to 25 minutes until heated through.
PER SERVING: 240.1 CALORIES; 6.2G FAT; 23.2G PROTEIN; 22.3G CARBOHYDRATES; 212MG CHOLESTEROL.

Crab Rice Chowder

6 servings

1 tablespoon vegetable oil
1 cup onion, chopped
1 cup mushrooms, sliced
½ teaspoon thyme
2 cups broccoli florette's, chopped coarsely
½ cup red bell pepper, chopped finely

2 cups reduced-fat chicken broth
2 cups skim milk
1 (17-oz.) can cream-style corn
1 (7½-oz.) can crab meat
3 cups cooked long-grain white rice
salt
pepper

ADVANCE STEPS:

Cook rice. Chop onions, red bell pepper and broccoli. Slice mushrooms.

PREPARATION:

In bottom of stockpot or Dutch oven, heat oil. Add onions, mushrooms and thyme. Cook, stirring frequently, until vegetables are tender. Add broccoli and bell pepper. Cook, stirring frequently, until broccoli begins to change to bright green and slightly soften. Remove from heat. Stir in broth, milk, corn, crab and rice. Season with salt and pepper. Cool. Place in labeled freezer bag; freeze.

TO SERVE:

Thaw. Pour into pot. Heat over medium heat, stirring frequently, just until heated through. Don't boil.

PER SERVING: 234.4 CALORIES; 3.4G FAT; 17.3G PROTEIN; 36.5G CARBOHYDRATES; 29MG CHOLESTEROL.

Crab Strata

6 servings

8 slices bread
1 (7½-oz.) can crab meat,
   drained and flaked
¼ cup celery, thinly sliced
1 green onion, thinly sliced
4-oz. (1 cup) reduced-fat
   cheddar cheese, sliced

5 eggs (or equivalent egg
   substitute)
2½ cups skim milk
½ teaspoon salt
1 tablespoon prepared mustard

ADVANCE PREP:

Cut off bread crusts. Slice celery and green onion. Grate 1 cup cheddar cheese.

PREPARATION:

Spray 9x13-inch baking dish with cooking spray. Arrange bread in bottom of
pan. In mixing bowl, combine crab, celery and onion; sprinkle evenly over
bread. Sprinkle cheese evenly over top of crab mixture. In bowl, beat together
eggs, milk, salt and
prepared mustard.
Cover, label and
freeze.

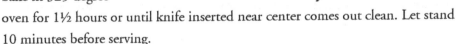

TO SERVE:

Thaw. Uncover and
bake in 325 degree
oven for 1½ hours or until knife inserted near center comes out clean. Let stand
10 minutes before serving.

*Note: This can be baked before freezing but needs to sit in refrigerator for at least
4 hours before baking. After baking, cool completely, label and freeze. To reheat,
thaw and bake in 325 degree oven for 25 minutes or until heated through.*

PER SERVING: 255.3 CALORIES; 6.1G FAT; 24.5G PROTEIN; 24.9G CARBOHYDRATES; 213MG CHOLESTEROL.

Crab-stuffed Manicotti

6 servings

6 large manicotti shells
1½ cups fat-free cottage cheese
4 garlic cloves, minced
1 teaspoon onion powder
1 (7½-oz.) can crab meat,
   drained and flaked
1 teaspoon Italian seasoning
1 teaspoon Dijon mustard

¼ teaspoon salt
¼ teaspoon pepper
1 tablespoon margarine
4 teaspoons flour
1 cup skim milk
dash bottled hot pepper sauce
¼ cup Parmesan cheese (for
   serving time)

ADVANCE PREP:

Cook manicotti according to package directions; drain. Rinse with cold water.
Let pasta sit in pan full of cold water until ready to use.

PREPARATION:

In large bowl, combine cottage cheese, garlic, onion powder, crab, Italian spice,
mustard, salt and pepper. In saucepan, melt margarine. Set aside. Add milk and
flour; cook and stir over medium-low heat until thick and bubbly. Stir 2
tablespoons of white sauce into crab mixture. Fill each manicotti shell with crab
mixture. Place in a 10x6x2″ baking dish. Stir hot pepper sauce into remaining
white sauce. Spoon over manicotti.

TO SERVE:

Thaw. Cover tightly; bake at 350 degrees for 25 minutes. Top with Parmesan
cheese.

PER SERVING: 287.4 CALORIES; 2.4G FAT; 23.8G PROTEIN; 41.5G CARBOHYDRATES; 37MG CHOLESTEROL.

Tuna Mini-Session

Crustless Tuna-Spinach Quiche
Italian Chowder
Tuna Mex Casserole

Tuna-Bean Pasta Salad
Tuna-Mac

Shopping List

MEAT
9 cans tuna fish

DAIRY
4-oz. reduced fat Monterey Jack
  cheese
1 cup egg substitute (or 3 eggs)
6 cups skim milk
1 cup 2% milk
¼ cup margarine
6-oz. grated reduced-fat cheddar
  cheese

BREAD / PASTA
2½ cups elbow macaroni
3 cups small pasta shells
dry bread crumbs

VEGETABLES
1 red bell pepper
2 garlic cloves
4 green onions
3 medium onions
3 large carrots
2 large tomatoes
1 bunch celery
1 bunch fresh parsley

CANNED / BOXED
1 can tomatoes with green chili
  peppers
2 cans Italian-style stewed tomatoes
2 (15-oz.) cans red kidney beans

SPICES

flour
salt
pepper
hot pepper sauce
parsley
bay leaf
oregano
mixed herbs
olive oil
white wine vinegar
lemon juice
Dijon-style mustard
cornstarch
dry mustard
paprika
basil
marjoram
thyme
cayenne (ground red pepper)

FROZEN
1 (10-oz.) package frozen spinach
3 cups frozen mixed vegetables
2 cups frozen peas and carrots

MISC.
cooking spray
white wine (or white grape juice)
baking powder
vegetable oil
1 box rye crackers

Preparation Instructions

VEGETABLE PREP:

1 cup frozen spinach—thawed and squeezed dry (squeeze in paper towels to remove last bit of moisture).

1 medium red bell pepper—chop.

3 medium onions—chop.

1 cup carrots—grate.

4 large ribs celery—chop.

4 green onions—slice.

2 garlic cloves—mince.

½ cup fresh parsley—chop

CHEESE PREP:

4-oz. (1 cup) reduced-fat Monterey Jack cheese—grate.

6-oz. (½ cup) reduced-fat cheddar cheese—grate.

MISC. PREP:

3½ cups elbow macaroni—cook according to directions until almost tender; drain.

Crustless Tuna-Spinach Quiche

6 servings

1 can (6 -oz.) water packed
   tuna, drained and flaked

4 oz. (1 cup) reduced-fat
   Monterey Jack cheese, grated

1 cup frozen spinach, thawed
   and squeezed dry

½ cup red bell pepper, chopped

½ cup onion, chopped

¼ cup flour

½ teaspoon salt (optional)

1 teaspoon baking powder

1 cup egg substitute (or 3 eggs)

1 cup 2% milk (or 8-oz. non-fat
   evaporated milk)

½ teaspoon hot pepper sauce

ADVANCE PREP:

Grate cheese. Chop red bell pepper and onion. Thaw frozen spinach and squeeze dry (squeeze in paper towels to remove last bits of moisture).

PREPARATION:

In mixing bowl, combine tuna, cheese, spinach, bell pepper, onion, flour, salt and baking powder. Place mixture in bottom of labeled one-gallon freezer bag. In same bowl, whisk together eggs (or egg substitute), milk and hot pepper sauce. Pour into freezer bag over tuna mixture. Remove air from bag. Label and freeze.

TO SERVE:

Thaw completely. Squeeze or shake bag to recombine quiche mixture, or pour into mixing bowl and stir to combine. Spray 9-inch pie plate with nonstick cooking spray. Empty quiche mixture into pie plate. Spread the larger ingredients evenly throughout the pie plate. Bake in preheated 350 degree oven for 40 - 50 minutes until knife inserted in center comes out clean. Important: let stand 10 minutes before slicing or serving. Cut into 6 equal wedges.

PER SERVING: 190.8 CALORIES; 6.9G FAT; 20.0G PROTEIN; 10.8 CARBOHYDRATES; 17MG CHOLESTEROL.

Tuna-Bean Pasta Salad

6 servings

Dressing:
½ cup olive oil
3 tablespoons white wine
  vinegar
1 tablespoon lemon juice
1 tablespoon Dijon mustard
2 (15-oz.) cans red kidney
  beans, drained and rinsed

2 (7-oz.) cans tuna, drained and
  flaked
4 green onions, sliced
1 tablespoon dried mixed herbs
For Serving Day:
3 cups small pasta shells,
  uncooked

ADVANCE PREP:
Slice green onions.

PREPARATION:
In medium bowl, mix first four ingredients together thoroughly. Stir in kidney beans, tuna, green onions and herbs. Pour into labeled freezer bag. Remove air and freeze.

TO SERVE:
Thaw bean/tuna mixture completely. Squeeze bag gently to recombine. Cook pasta shells according to package directions until just tender. Rinse thoroughly in cold water, drain. Place pasta shells in large mixing bowl. Stir bean/tuna mixture into pasta shells until coated. Serve as a salad main course, or as a side dish.

PER SERVING: 571.6 CALORIES; 20.0G FAT; 28.3G PROTEIN; 71.1G CARBOHYDRATES; 14MG CHOLESTEROL.

Italian Chowder

6 servings

2 cans tuna, drained
¼ cup olive oil
1 cup onions, chopped
1 cup carrots, grated
1 cup celery, chopped
½ cup parsley, fresh
2 cups dry white wine (or white grape juice)

1 bay leaf
2 cups canned Italian-style stewed tomatoes
2 teaspoons salt
½ teaspoon pepper
½ teaspoon dried oregano

On Serving Day:
4 cups water

ADVANCE PREP:
Chop onions and celery. Grate carrots.

PREPARATION:
Sauté onions, carrots, celery and parsley in olive oil for 10 minutes. Stir in wine and bay leaf; reduce heat to low. Cook 10 minutes. Cool. Add tomatoes, salt, pepper, oregano and tuna. Pour into labeled zip-top freezer bag. Remove air and freeze.

TO SERVE:
Thaw completely. Pour into large saucepan or Dutch oven. Add 4 cups water. Heat for 10 minutes over medium heat or until heated through.

PER SERVING: 235.9 CALORIES; 9.7G FAT; 13.6G PROTEIN; 12.3G CARBOHYDRATES; 14MG CHOLESTEROL.

Tuna Mac

6 servings

1 cup onion, chopped
½ cup celery, chopped
2 garlic cloves, minced
¼ cup margarine
½ cup cornstarch
1 teaspoon salt
½ teaspoon pepper
4 cups skim milk

2 cups elbow macaroni
4 oz. (1 cup) reduced-fat
    cheddar cheese, grated
2 cups frozen peas and carrots
½ teaspoon dry mustard
2 (7-oz.) cans tuna, drained and
    flaked

On Serving Day:
¼ cup dry bread crumbs
1 tablespoon margarine, melted
½ teaspoon paprika

ADVANCE PREP:

Cook macaroni according to package directions (until just tender). Chop onion and celery. Mince garlic. Grate cheese.

PREPARATION:

In medium saucepan, cook onion, celery and garlic in margarine until vegetables are tender. Stir in cornstarch, salt and pepper. Add milk, and cook over medium heat until thickened and bubbly, stirring frequently. Remove from heat. Stir in cheese, peas and carrots, dry mustard and macaroni into saucepan. Stir until cheese is melted. Fold in tuna. Cool in refrigerator. Place into labeled freezer bag. Remove air and freeze.

TO SERVE:

Thaw completely. Pour into 2-quart casserole. Sprinkle bread crumbs combined with melted butter and paprika over top. Bake uncovered in 375 degree oven for 35 - 40 minutes until heated through.

PER SERVING: 391.1 CALORIES; 11.1G FAT; 28.7G PROTEIN; 44.4G CARBOHYDRATES; 20MG CHOLESTEROL.

Tuna-Mex Casserole

6 servings

1½ cups elbow macaroni, uncooked

½ cup celery, sliced

½ cup onion, chopped

1½ teaspoons vegetable oil

1 10-oz. can tomatoes with green chili peppers, drained

2 cups skim milk

½ cup cornstarch

3 cups frozen mixed vegetables

½ cup (2 oz.) reduced-fat cheddar cheese, grated

½ teaspoon basil

¼ teaspoon marjoram

¼ teaspoon thyme

⅛ teaspoon cayenne

2 (7-oz.) cans tuna, drained and flaked

⅓ cup rye crackers, crushed

ADVANCE PREP:

Cook macaroni according to package directions until almost tender; drain. Slice celery. Chop onion. Grate cheese. /

PREPARATION:

In medium saucepan, cook celery and onion in oil until tender. Stir in tomatoes, milk and cornstarch. Cook over medium heat, stirring constantly, until slightly thickened. Remove from heat. Then combine in vegetables, cheese, basil, marjoram, thyme, red pepper and macaroni. Fold in tuna. Pour into labeled freezer bag. Remove air and freeze.

TO SERVE:

Thaw completely. Pour into 2-quart casserole. Bake at 350 degrees for one hour. Sprinkle with crushed crackers for last 10 minutes of baking time.

PER SERVING: 292.1 CALORIES; 2.7G FAT; 18.4G PROTEIN; 49.7G CARBOHYDRATES; 10MG CHOLESTEROL.

Pasta Mini-Session #1

Italian Pasta Bake
Linguini with Vegetables
Three Cheese Mac-n-Cheese
Italian Garden Pasta

Shopping List

DAIRY
2½ cups skim milk
Parmesan cheese
1 cup fat-free cottage cheese (or fat-free ricotta)
2-oz. fat-free cream cheese
2-oz. reduced-fat mozzarella cheese
6-oz. reduced-fat cheddar cheese
margarine
butter

BREAD / PASTA
1 pound dry pasta (any shape)
1 pound dry ziti pasta
3 cups elbow macaroni
⅓ cup Italian flavored bread crumbs
10-oz. linguine

VEGETABLES
2 medium onions
2 medium red onions

2½ pounds whole, fresh mushrooms
7 garlic cloves

CANNED / BOXED
3 (16-oz.) cans Italian-style stewed tomatoes
12-oz. non-fat evaporated milk
small can tomato paste

SPICES
basil
pepper
flour

FROZEN
10-oz. frozen spinach
3 cups frozen baby carrots
3 cups frozen sugar snap peas

MISC.
olive oil

Preparation Instructions

VEGETABLE PREP:

2 medium onions—chop.

7 garlic cloves—mince.

2 pounds mushrooms—slice.

1 large red onion—slice.

CHEESE PREP:

2-oz. (½ cup) reduced-fat mozzarella cheese—grate.

6-oz. (1½ cups) reduced-fat cheddar cheese—grate.

MISC. PREP:

3 cups elbow macaroni—cook according to package directions; rinse in cold
water; store in refrigerator in pan full of water until ready to use.

1 pound ziti macaroni—cook according to package directions; rinse in cold
water; store in refrigerator in pan full of water until ready to use.

frozen spinach—thaw and drain well.

Italian Pasta Bake

6 servings

1 cup onion, chopped
1 tablespoon olive oil
3 garlic cloves, minced
2 (15-oz.) cans Italian-style
stewed tomatoes, pureed
1 tablespoon basil

1 pound ziti macaroni,
uncooked
1 cup fat-free cottage cheese (or
fat-free ricotta)
¼ cup Parmesan cheese
2-oz. (½ cup) reduced-fat
mozzarella cheese, grated

ADVANCE PREP:

Cook ziti according to package directions but only until just tender (don't overcook). Rinse in cold water; store in refrigerator in pan full of cold water until ready to use. Chop onion. Mince garlic.

PREPARATION:

In large saucepan, sauté onion and garlic in hot oil until tender. Stir in tomatoes and basil, cook for 2 minutes. Remove from heat. In large mixing bowl, place cooked ziti, cottage cheese (or ricotta) and Parmesan cheese. Add tomato-onion mixture. Stir to combine. Place in labeled freezer bags. Place grated mozzarella in small freezer bag and attach to bag containing pasta mixture. Freeze both bags together.

TO SERVE:

Thaw. Pour ziti mixture into large casserole dish. Sprinkle with mozzarella. Bake at 350 degrees for 30 minutes or until heated through.

PER SERVING: 465.9 CALORIES; 5.9G FAT; 23.0G PROTEIN; 83.8G CARBOHYDRATES; 6MG CHOLESTEROL.

Linguini with Vegetables

6 servings

2 teaspoons olive oil
4 garlic cloves, minced
2 tablespoons butter
1½ cups mushrooms, sliced
1½ cups red onion, sliced
1½ cups non-fat evaporated
  milk

1 tablespoon tomato paste
3 cups frozen whole baby
  carrots
3 cups frozen sugar snap peas
10-oz. linguine, uncooked
¼ cup Parmesan cheese

ADVANCE PREP:

Mince garlic. Slice mushrooms and red onion.

PREPARATION:

In large skillet heat oil; add garlic and sauté over high heat until golden, 30 seconds to 1 minute. Using slotted spoon remove and discard garlic. In same skillet, melt butter; add mushroom and onion and sauté over high heat until crisp-tender. In large mixing bowl, combine milk and tomato paste and stir to combine; stir in mushroom-onion mixture, frozen carrots and snap peas. Pour into labeled freezer bags. Remove air and freeze.

TO SERVE:

Thaw completely. Cook linguine according to package directions. While pasta is cooking, pour sauce into skillet and heat over medium heat until heated through, stirring frequently to combine. When sauce is recombined, thickened and heated through, serve over hot linguine. Sprinkle with Parmesan cheese.

PER SERVING: 545.4 CALORIES; 16.0G FAT; 28.7G PROTEIN; 72.8G CARBOHYDRATES; 35MG CHOLESTEROL.

Three Cheese Mac-n-Cheese

6 servings

3 cups elbow macaroni, uncooked

¼ cup flour

⅛ teaspoon pepper

2½ cups skim milk

¼ cup Parmesan cheese

6-oz. (1½ cups) reduced-fat cheddar cheese, grated

2-oz. fat-free cream cheese, cubed

⅓ cup Italian flavored bread crumbs

1 tablespoon margarine, melted

ADVANCE PREP:

Prepare macaroni according to package directions; rinse in cold water; store in refrigerator in pan full of cold water until ready to use. Grate cheddar cheese.

PREPARATION:

Combine flour and pepper in large saucepan. Add ½ cup milk, whisk until smooth. Gradually add rest of milk, stirring briskly. Cook over medium heat until mixture just barely begins to boil. Remove from heat; add cheeses, stirring until melted. Stir in macaroni. Pour mixture into 9-inch square baking dish. Mix bread crumbs with margarine. Sprinkle over top of casserole. Wrap, label and freeze.

TO SERVE:

Thaw completely. Unwrap. Bake at 350 degrees for 30 minutes or until golden brown and bubbly.

PER SERVING: 294.4 CALORIES; 5.9G FAT; 22.8G PROTEIN; 36.6G CARBOHYDRATES; 15MG CHOLESTEROL.

Italian Garden Pasta

6 servings

10-oz. frozen spinach, thawed and well drained

1 pound dried macaroni (or other favorite pasta shape), save for serving day

3 tablespoons olive oil

1 pound mushrooms, sliced

1 medium onion, chopped

1 (16-oz.) can Italian-style stewed tomatoes, cut up into small pieces (and don't drain)

¼ cup Parmesan cheese (for serving day)

ADVANCE PREP:

Slice mushrooms. Chop onion. Thaw spinach. Drain well. Pat with dry paper towels to remove as much liquid as possible.

PREPARATION:

In large saucepan, heat olive oil. Add mushrooms and onions; cook until vegetables are softened. Remove from heat. Stir in Italian-style stewed tomatoes (and the tomato liquid). Add spinach. Stir until combined. Place in labeled freezer bag; freeze.

TO SERVE:

Thaw sauce. Cook pasta according to package directions. Heat sauce in large skillet just until heated through. Toss pasta with sauce. Sprinkle with Parmesan cheese.

PER SERVING: 405.7 CALORIES; 9.5G FAT; 14.7G PROTEIN; 66.8G CARBOHYDRATES; 3MG CHOLESTEROL.

Pasta Mini-Session #2

Spinach Ricotta Bows
Spaghetti Pie
Pasta with Vegetable Cheese Sauce
Cheese Manicotti
Florentine Shells
Creamy Penne

Shopping List

DAIRY
3 cups part-skim ricotta cheese
3½ cups fat-free cottage cheese
6-oz. (1½ cups) reduced-fat
  cheddar cheese
1½ cups Parmesan cheese
3 tablespoons margarine
4 eggs
12-oz. reduced-fat mozzarella
  cheese

BREAD / PASTA
1 pound bow-tie pasta
6-oz. dry spaghetti noodles
spinach fettuccini (to serve six)
12 manicotti shells
18 large macaroni shells
10-oz. penne pasta (or rigatoni)

VEGETABLES
3½ medium onions
2 green onions
9 garlic cloves
1½ cups carrots
7 cups broccoli flowerets
12 sun-dried tomato halves (not
  packed in oil)

3 cups cauliflower flowerets

CANNED / BOXED
2 (16-oz.) can Italian-style stewed
  tomatoes
1 (8-oz.) can tomato sauce
1 (6-oz.) can tomato paste
32-oz. (4 cups) spaghetti sauce
16 oz. non-fat evaporated milk

SPICES
basil
oregano
garlic powder
thyme
salt
pepper
nutmeg
bay leaf
parsley
sugar
flour
olive oil
vegetable oil

FROZEN
3 (10-oz.) packages frozen spinach

Preparation Instructions

2 (10-oz.) packages frozen spinach—thaw and drain; pat dry with paper towels to remove as much liquid as possible.

1 large onion—chop.

1 large onion—slice thinly.

2 green onions—slice thinly.

1½ cups carrots—slice thinly.

7 cups broccoli flowerets—cut into large chunks.

3 cups cauliflower flowerets—cut into large chunks.

9 garlic cloves —mince.

12 sun-dried tomato halves—slice.

CHEESE PREP:

12-oz. reduced-fat mozzarella cheese—grate.

4-oz. reduced-fat cheddar cheese—grate.

MISC. PREP:

6-oz. dry spaghetti noodles—cook according to package directions until just tender; drain and rinse in cold water; store in large pan full of water in refrigerator until ready to use.

12 manicotti shells—cook according to package directions; rinse in cold water; store in large pan full of cold water until ready to use.

18 large macaroni shells—cook shells according to package directions; drain and rinse in cold water; store in large pan full of cold water in refrigerator until ready to use.

Spinach Ricotta Bows

6 servings

10-oz. frozen spinach, thawed
and well-drained

2 tablespoons olive oil

1 medium onion, chopped

4 garlic cloves, minced

½ cup water

1½ cups part-skim ricotta
cheese (or fat-free small curd
cottage cheese)

½ teaspoon salt

¼ teaspoon pepper

dash nutmeg

1 pound bow-tie pasta, save for
serving day

¼ cup Parmesan cheese

ADVANCE PREP:

Thaw and drain spinach. Pat dry with paper towels to remove as much liquid as possible. Chop onion. Mince garlic.

PREPARATION:

In large skillet, heat olive oil. Add onion and garlic; cook until onion is softened. Add ½ cup water; bring to boil. Remove from heat. Stir in spinach, ricotta cheese, salt, pepper and nutmeg. Place in labeled freezer bag; freeze.

TO SERVE:

Thaw. Cook pasta according to package directions. Reheat sauce over low heat until heated through and recombined, stirring gently and frequently. Spoon sauce over pasta and toss gently.

PER SERVING: 404.6 CALORIES; 6.9G FAT; 21.9G PROTEIN; 63.8G CARBOHYDRATES; 13MG CHOLESTEROL.

Spaghetti Pie

6 servings

6-oz. dry spaghetti noodles
2 tablespoons margarine
½ cup Parmesan cheese
2 eggs, beaten
1 teaspoon vegetable oil
½ cup onion, chopped
1 (16-oz.) can Italian-style
   stewed tomatoes, undrained

1 (6-oz.) can tomato paste
1 teaspoon sugar
1 teaspoon oregano
½ clove garlic, minced
1 cup fat-free cottage cheese
4-oz. reduced-fat cheddar
   cheese, grated (or: mozzarella,
   Monterey Jack)

ADVANCED PREP:

Chop onion. Mince garlic. Cook spaghetti noodles according to package directions. Drain. Stir margarine into hot noodles until melted. Stir in Parmesan cheese and beaten eggs. Spray 9-inch pie plate with cooking spray. Form pasta mixture into a crust-shape in bottom and up sides of pie plate. Store covered in refrigerator until ready to use.

PREPARATION:

In a skillet, heat vegetable oil. Cook onion until softened. Add tomatoes, tomato paste, sugar, oregano and garlic. Heat through. Spread cottage cheese over bottom of spaghetti crust. Top with tomato mixture. Sprinkle grated cheese over all. Cover pie with foil; label and freeze.

TO SERVE:

Thaw. Bake covered for 25 minutes at 350 degrees. Remove foil and bake for five more minutes or until cheese is lightly browned.

PER SERVING: 281.9 CALORIES; 9.0G FAT; 18.1G PROTEIN; 33.3G CARBOHYDRATES; 80MG CHOLESTEROL.

Pasta with Vegetable Cheese Sauce

6 servings

2 teaspoons olive oil
1½ cups onion, sliced thinly
1½ cups carrot, sliced thinly
3 garlic cloves, minced
1 tablespoon flour
3 cups water
3 cups broccoli flowerets

3 cups cauliflower flowerets
1½ cups fat-free ricotta cheese
12 sun-dried tomato halves,
   sliced (not packed in oil)
spinach fettuccine to serve six
   (for serving day)

ADVANCE PREP:

Slice onion and carrot. Mince garlic. Cut up broccoli and cauliflower into large
chunks. Slice sun-dried tomatoes.

PREPARATION:

In skillet, heat oil and add onion, carrot and garlic. Cook over medium heat,
stirring frequently until onion and carrot slices are softened. Sprinkle with flour.
Stir and cook for 1 minute. Add water, broccoli and cauliflower. Reduce heat to
low; cover and simmer until broccoli and cauliflower are just beginning to get
tender. Stir in cheese and tomatoes. Stir over low heat for 1 minute. Remove
from heat. Cool. Place in labeled freezer bag; freeze.

TO SERVE:

Thaw. Cook spinach fettuccine according to package directions. Heat vegetable
sauce over low heat until heated through. Serve vegetable sauce spooned over
hot spinach noodles.

PER SERVING: 309.3 CALORIES; 2.7G FAT; 18.9G PROTEIN; 53.3G CARBOHYDRATES; 10MG CHOLESTEROL.

Cheese Manicotti

6 servings

½ cup onion, chopped
1 clove garlic, minced
1 tablespoon vegetable oil
1 (16-oz.) can Italian-style
   stewed tomatoes, cut up
1 (8-oz.) can tomato sauce
⅓ cup water
1 teaspoon sugar
1 teaspoon oregano
1 teaspoon thyme

¼ teaspoon salt
1 bay leaf
12 manicotti shells
2 eggs, beaten
1½ cups fat-free cottage cheese
8-oz. (2 cups) reduced-fat
   mozzarella cheese, grated
¼ cup Parmesan cheese
¼ cup parsley
dash pepper

ADVANCE PREP:

Chop onion. Mince garlic. Grate mozzarella cheese. Cook manicotti shells according to package directions. Rinse in cold water. Store in large pan of cold water until ready to use.

PREPARATION:

In large saucepan, heat salad oil; add onion and garlic; cook until onion is softened. Stir in tomatoes, tomato sauce, water, sugar, oregano, thyme, salt and bay leaf. Bring to boil. Simmer, uncovered, for 45 minutes. In mixing bowl, combine eggs, cottage cheese, mozzarella cheese, Parmesan cheese, parsley and pepper. Drain manicotti shells. Spoon cheese mixture into manicotti. Pour half of tomato mixture into 13x9-inch baking dish. Place stuffed shells into pan; pour remaining sauce over top of shells. Cover with foil. Label and freeze.

TO SERVE:

Thaw. Bake, covered, in 350 degree oven for 45 minutes or until hot and bubbly.

PER SERVING: 410.5 CALORIES; 7.1G FAT; 32.9G PROTEIN; 54.1G CARBOHYDRATES; 86MG CHOLESTEROL.

Florentine Shells

6 servings

18 large macaroni shells
1 (10-oz.) package frozen
   spinach, thawed and well-
   drained
4-oz. (1 cup) reduced-fat
   mozzarella cheese, grated
1 cup fat-free cottage cheese
¼ cup Parmesan cheese
2 green onions, thinly sliced

1 tablespoon parsley
1 teaspoon basil
¼ teaspoon salt
¼ teaspoon nutmeg
¼ teaspoon pepper
4 cups spaghetti sauce
   (homemade or commercially
   prepared)

ADVANCE PREP:

Grate mozzarella cheese. Slice green onions. Cook macaroni shells according to package directions. Drain, rinse in cold water. Store in large pan of cold water until ready to use.

PREPARATION:

In large bowl, combine spinach, mozzarella cheese, cottage cheese, Parmesan cheese, green onions, parsley, basil, salt, nutmeg and pepper. Drain macaroni shells. Spray 9x13-inch baking dish with cooking spray. Fill each macaroni shell with ¼ cup spinach/cheese mixture; place filled shells into baking dish. After all shells are filled, pour spaghetti sauce evenly over shells. Cover with foil; label and freeze.

TO SERVE:

Thaw. Bake in 350 degree oven for 35 minutes or until hot and bubbly. Let set 10 minutes before serving.

PER SERVING: 486.2 CALORIES; 10.1G FAT; 25.0G PROTEIN; 76.6G CARBOHYDRATES; 8MG CHOLESTEROL.

Creamy Penne

6 servings

3 teaspoons garlic powder
4 cups broccoli florette's
10-oz. penne pasta
1 tablespoon margarine
2 cups non-fat evaporated milk
2 tablespoons flour

4-oz. (1 cup) reduced-fat
  cheddar cheese, grated
¼ cup Parmesan cheese
¼ teaspoon salt
½ teaspoon pepper

ADVANCE PREP:

Cut broccoli into bite-sized chunks. Grate cheese. Mince garlic.

PREPARATION:

Steam broccoli until just tender. Set aside. Rinse in cold water. In large skillet, melt margarine over medium heat. Stir in evaporated milk and flour. With wire whisk, stir constantly until mixture is bubbling and thickened. Stir in garlic powder. Reduce heat to low. Add cheddar cheese, Parmesan cheese, salt and pepper. Stir constantly until cheese melts. Remove from heat. Stir in broccoli. Cool. Pour into labeled freezer bag; freeze.

TO SERVE:

Thaw. Cook penne according to package directions. Drain. Reheat broccoli/cheese sauce over low heat until heated through and recombined. Stir in a small amount of milk if too thick. Add pasta to sauce. Stir gently to combine. Serve.

PER SERVING: 320.9 CALORIES; 4.0G FAT; 20.3G PROTEIN; 51.1 CARBOHYDRATES; 8MG CHOLESTEROL.

Tofu Mini-Session #1

Broccoli Tofu Quiche
Tofu Fried Rice
Tofu Burgers / Loaves / Balls
Enchilada Casserole

Shopping List

DAIRY
4-oz. Monterey Jack cheese

BREAD / PASTA
12 corn tortillas
oatmeal
wheat germ
regular rice

VEGETABLES
1 green bell pepper
3 cups broccoli
3 large onions
2 green onions
4 pounds tofu
3 garlic cloves
2 celery ribs

CANNED / BOXED
½ cup sliced black olives

SPICES
basil
catsup
chili powder
cumin
flour
garlic powder
mustard, dry
onion powder
oregano
parsley
pepper
salt

MISC.
lemon juice
soy sauce
vegetable oil

Preparation Instructions

TOFU PREP:

1 pound tofu—drain and crumble. Squeeze excess water from tofu or place in colander inside larger bowl in refrigerator overnight to drain. After drained, crumble into small pieces.

1 pound tofu—mash.

½ pound tofu—cut into ½-inch cubes.

VEGETABLE PREP:

3 medium onions—chop.

1 green pepper—chop.

2 celery ribs—slice.

2 green onions—slice.

3 cups broccoli—cut into bite-sized pieces. Steam broccoli until tender.

3 garlic cloves—mince.

CHEESE PREP:

½ cup reduced-fat Monterey Jack cheese—grate.

MISC. PREP:

Rice—prepare 3 cups of regular cooked rice (not instant).

12 corn tortillas—slice into 1-inch slices.

Broccoli Tofu Quiche

6 servings

3 cups cooked broccoli, cut up
2 tablespoons vegetable oil
1 cup onion, chopped
3 garlic cloves, minced
1 pound tofu (divided in half)

2 tablespoons lemon juice
1 tablespoon dry mustard
1 teaspoon salt
¼ teaspoon pepper
1 tablespoon flour

ADVANCE PREP:

Cut up broccoli. Steam broccoli until tender. Set aside. Chop onion. Mince garlic.

PREPARATION:

In large skillet, sauté oil, onion and garlic until onion is softened. Remove from heat. Divide tofu into two equal portions. Crumble one half and set aside. Place other  half in blender or food processor. Add lemon juice, dry mustard, salt, pepper and flour. Process until smooth. Pour into skillet with onion and garlic. Stir to combine. Fold in crumbled tofu and broccoli. Spray 9-inch pie plate with cooking spray. Pour mixture into sprayed pie plate. Bake at 350 degrees for 30 minutes. Remove from oven. Cool. Wrap with foil. Label and freeze.

TO SERVE:

Thaw. Uncover and bake in 350 degree oven for 15 - 20 minutes or until heated through.

Note: You can substitute other cooked vegetables for the broccoli. Prepare as usual.
PER SERVING: 132.0 CALORIES; 8.6G FAT; 8.2G PROTEIN; 8.1G CARBOHYDRATES;0MG CHOLESTEROL.

Tofu Fried Rice

6 servings

3 cups cooked rice
1 large onion, chopped
1 green pepper, chopped
2 celery ribs, sliced
2 green onions, sliced

½ pound tofu, cut into ½-inch cubes
2 tablespoon oil
2 tablespoons soy sauce

ADVANCE PREP:

Cook rice according to package directions. Chop onion and green pepper. Slice celery and green onions. Cut tofu into ½-inch cubes.

PREPARATION:

In large skillet, heat oil over high heat. Add 1 tablespoon soy sauce and tofu; sauté for 1 minute. Remove tofu from skillet. Stir in onion, green pepper and celery. Sauté for 3 minutes or until vegetables are softened. Stir in cooked rice, 1 tablespoon soy sauce, and the tofu cubes. Sauté until rice is browned. Stir in green onion. Remove from heat. Cool. Pour into labeled freezer bag; freeze.

TO SERVE:

Thaw. In large skillet, heat 1 tablespoon vegetable oil over medium-high heat. Add rice mixture. Sauté until heated through.

PER SERVING: 223.0 CALORIES; 6.8G FAT; 7.3G PROTEIN; 34.3G CARBOHYDRATES; 0MG CHOLESTEROL.

Tofu Burgers / Loaves*** / Balls***

1 pound tofu, mashed
½ cup regular oatmeal
½ cup Wheat germ
2 tablespoons onion powder
1 tablespoon parsley, chopped

1 teaspoon salt
½ teaspoon basil
½ teaspoon oregano
½ teaspoon garlic powder
2 tablespoons vegetable oil

ADVANCE PREP:

Mash tofu.

PREPARATION:

In large mixing bowl, combine first nine ingredients. Shape into eight patties. Spray cookie sheet with cooking spray. Arrange patties in single layer on cookie sheet. Place in freezer until frozen solid. Remove patties from cookie sheet and place into labeled freezer bag; seal and freeze.

TO SERVE:

Remove frozen patties from bag and place on cookie sheet to thaw. After completely thawed, brown patties in large skillet in 2 tablespoons hot vegetable oil, turning once. Serve on buns with hamburger fixings.

Other options for this recipe:

Tofu "Meat" Balls: shape into 20 balls and brown in large skillet in ½ cup hot oil.

Tofu "Meat" Loaf: spray a loaf pan with cooking oil; press mixture into pan; bake at 350 degrees for 30 minutes. Spread • cup catsup over top of loaf during last ten minutes of baking time. Let set for 10 minutes before slicing.

PER SERVING: 167.7 CALORIES; 9.6G FAT; 9.8G PROTEIN; 13.1G CARBOHYDRATES; 0MG CHOLESTEROL.

Enchilada Casserole

6 servings

1 pound tofu, well-drained and crumbled

12 corn tortillas, sliced into 1-inch slices

2 tablespoons oil

1 cup onion, chopped

3 tablespoons chili powder

3 tablespoons flour

½ teaspoon garlic powder

½ teaspoon cumin

1 teaspoon salt

4 cups water

4-oz. (1 cup) reduced-fat Monterey Jack cheese, grate

½ cup black olives, sliced

ADVANCE PREP:

Squeeze excess water from tofu or place in colander inside larger bowl in refrigerator overnight to drain. After drained, crumble into small pieces. Chop onions. Slice tortillas into 1-inch slices.

PREPARATION:

In large skillet, sauté onion in hot oil until softened. Remove from heat. In mixing bowl, combine chili powder, flour, garlic powder, cumin and salt. Stir spice and flour mixture into skillet with onion and oil. Gradually add 4 cups water, stirring constantly to combine into thin, smooth gravy. Return to heat and bring to boil, stirring frequently. As soon as mixture boils, remove gravy from heat. Cover bottom of 9x9-inch square baking dish with ½ the gravy. Place ½ tortilla strips over gravy. Sprinkle tofu crumbles over tortillas; cover tofu with remaining tortilla strips and second ½ of gravy. Sprinkle with Monterey Jack cheese and black olives. Cover pan with foil; label and freeze.

TO SERVE:

Thaw. Bake, uncovered, in 350 degree oven for 20 minutes or until hot and bubbly.

PER SERVING: 307.9 CALORIES; 13.5G FAT; 15.8G PROTEIN; 33.7G CARBOHYDRATES; 7MG CHOLESTEROL.

Tofu Mini-Session #2

Tofu and Spinach Lasagna
Tamale Pie
Stuffed Shells
Tofu Sloppy Joes

Shopping List

DAIRY
4-oz. mozzarella cheese
2 eggs
2 cups skim milk

BREAD / PASTA
12 jumbo macaroni shells
16 oz. package lasagna noodles

VEGETABLES
4 pounds tofu
2 bunches fresh spinach
3 large onions
5 garlic cloves
3 large green bell peppers
parsley

CANNED / BOXED
5 cups prepared spaghetti sauce
1 (16-oz.) can diced tomatoes
2 (15-oz.) can tomato sauce
1 (8-oz.) can tomato paste
1 (6-oz.) can chopped green chilies
½ cup sliced black olives

SPICES
baking powder
baking soda
basil
chili powder
corn meal
cumin
flour
garlic powder
onion powder
oregano
sage
salt
sugar
bay leaves

FROZEN
10-oz. package frozen corn kernels

MISC.
olive oil
soy sauce
vegetable oil

Preparation Instructions

TOFU PREP:

1 pound tofu—drain slightly (don't squeeze out excess water); place in blender or food processor; blend until smooth. Spoon into mixing bowl; add spinach, oregano and basil; mix well. Store in refrigerator until ready to use.

1 pound tofu—drain well and cut into ½-inch cubes.

1 pound tofu—drain; mash with potato masher.

1 pound tofu—drain well and crumble into small pieces.

VEGETABLE PREP:

2 bunches fresh spinach (or 10-oz. package frozen; thawed and well drained)—rinse fresh spinach in cold water; cut off thick stems; keep water clinging to leaves; place in large stockpot; heat, covered, over high heat; stir frequently until spinach is soft; drain and squeeze out excess liquid.

2 medium green bell peppers—chop.

3 medium onions—chop.

5 garlic cloves—mince.

¼ cup fresh parsley—chop.

CHEESE PREP:

4-oz. reduced-fat mozzarella cheese—grate.

MISC. PREP:

12 jumbo macaroni shells—cook macaroni shells according to package direction until just soft; drain and rinse gently in cold water; store in large pan full of cold water in refrigerator until ready to use.

Tofu and Spinach Lasagna

8 servings

Sauce:

¼ cup water

¼ cup green pepper, chopped

½ cup onion, chopped

3 cloves garlic, minced

2 bay leaves, crushed

1 teaspoon basil

1 (16-oz.) can tomato sauce

1 (8-oz) can tomato paste

2 additional cups water

Filling:

1 pound tofu

2 bunches fresh spinach (or 10-oz. package frozen spinach)

1 teaspoon oregano

½ teaspoon basil

pinch of sage

1 (16-oz.) package lasagna noodles, uncooked

ADVANCE PREP:

Chop green pepper and onion. Mince garlic. Rinse fresh spinach in cold water. Cut off thick stems. Keep the water clinging to the leaves. Place in large stockpot. Heat covered over high heat, stirring frequently until spinach is soft. Drain spinach and squeeze out excess liquid. Set aside. Drain tofu slightly (don't squeeze out excess water). Place in blender container or food processor. Blend until smooth, stopping to scrape sides of container frequently. Spoon blended tofu into mixing bowl. Add spinach, oregano, sage and basil. Mix well. Store tofu and spinach in separate covered bowls in refrigerator until ready to use.

PREPARATION:

In large saucepan, combine ¼ cup water, green pepper, onion and garlic. Heat to boiling. Turn down heat to medium-low and simmer until soft, stirring frequently. Stir in crushed bay leaves, basil, tomato sauce, tomato paste and 2 cups water. Simmer for 15 minutes. Remove from heat. To assemble, spread 1 cup sauce over bottom of 9x13-inch pan. Top with ⅓ of the uncooked noodles, then 1 more cup of sauce. Spoon the tofu mixture by dollops over top of sauce. Add a second layer of noodles, followed by 1 cup sauce, and then spoon in the remaining tofu mixture. Add a third layer of noodles, pressing down firmly all over the lasagna. Spoon the remaining sauce over noodles, making sure that the noodles are completely covered with sauce. Wrap, label and freeze.

TO SERVE:

Thaw completely. Preheat oven to 350 degrees. Bake
covered for 40 minutes. Uncover lasagna and continue baking 15 more minutes.
Let stand 10 minutes before serving. Cut into squares to serve.

Tamale Pie

6 servings

1 pound tofu, well-drained and cut
  into ½-inch cubes

2 tablespoons oil

1 cup green pepper, chopped

1 cup onion, chopped

2 garlic cloves, minced

2 tablespoons chili powder

½ teaspoon cumin

½ teaspoon salt

½ teaspoon oregano

1 (16-oz.) can diced tomatoes

1 (15-oz.) can tomato sauce

1 (10-oz.) package frozen corn
  kernels

1 (6-oz.) can chopped green
  chilies

½ cup black olives, sliced

For Cornbread Topping: (a box of cornbread mix can be substituted)

2 cups cornmeal

½ cup flour

1 teaspoon salt

½ teaspoon baking soda

½ teaspoon baking powder

1 tablespoon sugar

2 eggs, beaten

1 tablespoon vegetable oil

2 cups skim milk

ADVANCE PREP:

Squeeze excess water from tofu or place in colander inside larger bowl in refrigerator overnight to drain. After drained, cut into ½-inch cubes. Chop green pepper and onion. Mince garlic.

PREPARATION:

In large skillet, sauté green pepper, onion and garlic in hot oil until almost softened. Stir in tofu, chili powder, cumin, salt and oregano; sauté for 2 minutes. Remove from heat. Stir in tomatoes, tomato sauce, frozen corn, green chilies and black olives. Spray 9x13-inch casserole dish with cooking spray; pour mixture into pan. In medium mixing bowl, combine cornmeal, flour, salt, baking soda and baking powder. In separate large mixing bowl, combine sugar, eggs, oil and milk. Gradually stir dry cornmeal mixture into milk and egg mixture. Stir until smooth but don't over mix. Pour corn meal mixture over top of tofu mixture in casserole dish. Cover with foil; label and freeze.

TO SERVE:

Thaw. Bake in 350 degree oven for 30 minutes or until cornbread topping is cooked and browned. PER SERVING: 502.7 CALORIES; 15.2G FAT; 20,1G PROTEIN; 76.0G CARBOHYDRATES; 73MG CHOLESTEROL.

Stuffed Shells

6 servings

12 jumbo macaroni shells
1 pound tofu, mashed
4-oz. (1 cup) reduced-fat
   mozzarella cheese, grated
¼ cup fresh parsley, chopped
2 tablespoons onion powder
1½ teaspoon salt

½ teaspoon garlic powder
½ teaspoon basil
3 cups spaghetti sauce
   (homemade or commercially
   prepared)
½ cup water

ADVANCE PREP:

Grate cheese. Mash tofu. Cook macaroni shells according to package directions. Rinse in cold water. Place in large pan of cold water until ready to use.

PREPARATION:

In large bowl, combine mashed tofu, cheese, parsley, onion powder, salt, garlic powder and basil. Spread ½ spaghetti sauce over bottom of 9x9-inch pan. Drain macaroni shells; fill each shell with ¼ cup tofu mixture; place into pan. Stir ½ water into remaining sauce and pour sauce over shells. Cover with foil; label and freeze.

TO SERVE:

Thaw. Bake in 350 degree oven for 30 minutes or until bubbly.
PER SERVING: 441.5 CALORIES; 10.5G FAT; 22.1G PROTEIN; 66.7G CARBOHYDRATES; 3MG CHOLESTEROL.

Tofu Sloppy Joes

6 servings

2 tablespoons oil
1 cup onion, chopped
1 cup green pepper, chopped
1 pound tofu, crumbled
2 tablespoons soy sauce

2 cups spaghetti sauce
(homemade or commercially prepared)
1 tablespoon chili powder

ADVANCE PREP:

Chop onion and green pepper. Crumble tofu.

PREPARATION:

In large skillet, sauté onion and green pepper in hot oil until softened. In mixing bowl, combine crumbled tofu and soy sauce. Add to onion and green pepper and continue frying until tofu begins to brown. Remove from heat. Stir in spaghetti sauce and chili powder. Place in labeled freezer bag; seal and freeze.

TO SERVE:

Thaw. Heat tofu mixture in large skillet until heated through. Serve on hamburger buns.

PER SERVING: 209.9 CALORIES; 12.4G FAT; 8.6G PROTEIN; 19.2G CARBOHYDRATES; 0MG CHOLESTEROL.

Cooked Beans Mini-Session

Pasta e Fagioli
Bean Casserole
Couscous Bean Paella

Veggie Bean Chili
Black Beans and Rice
Mexican Noodle Bake
Minestrone Soup

Shopping List

DAIRY
1 cup non-fat plain yogurt
8-oz. reduced-fat cheddar cheese
Parmesan cheese

BREAD / PASTA
4 cups dry elbow macaroni
1 ½ cups couscous
2 cups long grain rice

VEGETABLES
7 large onions
2 large green bell peppers
1 small red bell pepper
4 large stalks celery
6 large carrots
10 garlic cloves
1 lime
10-oz. potatoes
small head cabbage

CANNED / BOXED
5 (15-oz) cans white beans
6 (15-oz.) cans red kidney beans
4 (15-oz.) cans black beans
1 (15-oz.) can pinto beans
1 (16-oz.) can vegetable broth
5 (16-oz.) cans Italian-style stewed
  tomatoes
2 (16-oz.) cans diced tomatoes
1 (4-oz.) can tomato paste
1 (16-oz.) can tomato sauce
20-oz. canned vegetable broth
1 (10-oz.) can artichoke hearts
  (plain, not marinated)

32-oz. salsa (mild to hot, according
  to taste)
24-oz. tomato juice (or   V-8™)
1 package taco seasoning mix

SPICES
flour
rosemary
basil
cayenne
parsley
salt
pepper
bay leaf
marjoram
parsley
saffron
dry mustard
chili powder
red pepper flakes
cumin
oregano

FROZEN
1 cup frozen peas
1 cup frozen cut green
beans
20-oz. frozen whole corn kernels

MISC.
olive oil
molasses
soy sauce

Preparation Instructions

VEGETABLE PREP:

7 cups onion—chop.

2½ cups green bell pepper—chop.

1 cup red bell pepper—chop.

½ cup celery—chop.

1 cup celery—slice.

5 large carrots—slice thinly.

10 garlic cloves—mince.

10-oz. potatoes—pare and dice; store in pan full of cold water in refrigerator until ready to use.

2 cups cabbage—shred.

CHEESE PREP:

8-oz. reduced-fat cheddar cheese—grate.

MISC. PREP:

2 cups dry elbow macaroni—cook according to package directions until just tender; drain and rinse in cold water; store in large pan full of cold water in refrigerator until ready to use.

Pasta e Fagioli

6 servings

2 cans white beans, drained
1 (16-oz.) can vegetable broth
2 tablespoons olive oil
1 cup onion, chopped
½ cup green pepper, chopped
½ cup celery, sliced
1 cup carrots, thinly sliced
2 tablespoons flour
½ teaspoon rosemary
1 teaspoon basil

¼ teaspoon cayenne
4 tablespoons parsley
1 (16-oz.) can Italian-style
   stewed tomatoes
1 (4-oz.) can tomato paste
1 teaspoon salt
½ teaspoon pepper
3 garlic cloves, minced
1 cup elbow macaroni, dry
4 cups water (for serving day)

ADVANCE PREP:

Chop onion and green pepper. Slice celery and carrots. Mince garlic.

PREPARATION:

In large skillet, sauté onion, green pepper, celery and carrots in hot olive oil until softened. Remove from heat. Stir in flour, rosemary, basil, cayenne, parsley, stewed tomatoes, tomato paste, salt, pepper and garlic. Add dry macaroni, white beans and broth. Don't add water at this time. Place in labeled freezer bag; seal and freeze.

TO SERVE:

Thaw. Place in stockpot. Add 4 cups water. Heat until boiling. Make sure macaroni is cooked through. Serve.

PER SERVING: 397.3 CALORIES; 6.5G FAT; 20.6G PROTEIN; 67.8G CARBOHYDRATES; 1MG CHOLESTEROL.

Bean Casserole

6 servings

2 tablespoon olive oil
1 cup onion, chopped
2 garlic cloves, minced
1 cup green pepper, chopped
2 (16-oz.) cans Italian-style
stewed tomatoes, drained and
chopped

1 teaspoon salt
½ teaspoon pepper
1 bay leaf
½ teaspoon marjoram
4 tablespoons parsley
2 cans kidney beans, rinsed and
drained

ADVANCE PREP:

Chop onion and green pepper. Mince garlic.

PREPARATION:

In large skillet, sauté onion, garlic and green pepper in hot oil until softened. Remove from heat. Stir in tomatoes, salt, pepper, bay leaf, marjoram and parsley. Stir in beans. Place into labeled freezer bag; seal and freeze.

TO SERVE:

Thaw. Place into 2-quart casserole dish. Bake, covered, in 325 degree oven for 1 hour.

Note: Can be baked before freezing. Freeze in baking dish; reheat by baking in 325 degree oven for 20 minutes or until heated through.

PER SERVING: 151.0 CALORIES; 5.0G FAT; 6.0G PROTEIN; 22.7G CARBOHYDRATES; 0MG CHOLESTEROL.

Couscous Bean Paella

6 servings

2 teaspoons olive oil
1 cup onion, chopped
1 cup red bell pepper, chopped
  coarsely
2¼ cups canned vegetable
  broth
⅛ teaspoon saffron

1 can artichoke hearts (*not* the
  marinated kind)
1 cup frozen peas
1½ cups couscous
1 (15-oz.) can black beans,
  drained and rinsed
one lime (cut into wedges on
  serving day)

ADVANCE PREP:

Chop onion and red bell pepper.

PREPARATION:

In large skillet, sauté onion and red bell pepper in hot oil until softened.
Remove from heat. Stir in saffron, vegetable broth, artichoke hearts, peas,
couscous and black beans. Pour into labeled freezer bag; seal and freeze.

TO SERVE:

Thaw. Place into large saucepan; reheat over medium heat until heated through.
Serve with lime wedges.

PER SERVING: 413.3 CALORIES; 4.2G FAT; 18.6G PROTEIN; 77.4G CARBOHYDRATES; 1MG CHOLESTEROL.

Veggie Bean Chili

6 servings

¼ cup molasses
2 teaspoons dry mustard
2 teaspoons soy sauce
½ cup water
2 garlic cloves, minced
2 medium carrots, sliced
2 cups onion, chopped
1 tablespoon chili powder

1 teaspoons red pepper flakes
1 (16-oz.) can diced tomatoes
1 (15-oz.) can pinto beans, drained and rinsed
2 (15-oz.) cans red kidney beans, drained and rinsed
1 cup non-fat plain yogurt (for serving day)

ADVANCE PREP:
Mince garlic cloves. Slice carrots. Chop onions.

PREPARATION:
In small bowl, combine molasses, mustard and soy sauce. In large skillet, cook in ½ cup water over medium heat: garlic, carrots, onion, chili powder and red pepper flakes until carrots are almost tender. Uncover and cook until any liquid evaporates. Remove from heat. Stir in molasses mixture; then stir in tomatoes, pinto beans and kidney beans. Pour into labeled freezer bag; seal and freeze.

TO SERVE:
Thaw. Place into large saucepan. Cook over medium heat until heated through. Serve with dollop of plain yogurt.

PER SERVING: 284.5 CALORIES; 1.4G FAT; 14.6G PROTEIN; 56.0G CARBOHYDRATES; 1MG CHOLESTEROL.

Black Beans and Rice

6 servings

2 (15-oz.) cans black beans, drained and rinsed

20-oz. frozen corn kernels

2 cups long grain rice, uncooked

32-oz. salsa (mild to hot, according to your taste)

3 cups tomato juice

½ teaspoon cumin

½ teaspoon oregano

4-oz. (1 cup) reduced-fat cheddar cheese, grated

ADVANCE PREP:

Rinse and drain beans. Grate cheese.

PREPARATION:

In large bowl, combine all ingredients (except cheese). Pour into 13x9-inch casserole dish; bake for 1 hour at 375 degrees. Remove from oven. Cool; wrap with foil; label and freeze. Place grated cheese into small bag and attach to casserole dish. Thaw. Sprinkle with grated cheese. Cook at 350 degrees for 15 - 20 minutes or until cheese is melted and beans and rice are heated through.

PER SERVING: 471.3 CALORIES; 3.0G FAT; 25.7G PROTEIN; 90.4G CARBOHYDRATES; 4MG CHOLESTEROL.

Mexican Noodle Bake

6 servings

2 tablespoons vegetable oil
1 cup onion, chopped
1 cup green pepper, chopped
1 cup celery, sliced
1 package taco seasoning
1 (15-oz.) can black beans,
    drained and rinsed

1 (15-oz.) can red kidney beans,
    undrained
1 (16-oz.) tomato sauce
1 (16-oz.) can diced tomatoes
2 cups elbow macaroni, dry
4-oz. (1 cup) reduced-fat
    cheddar cheese, grated

ADVANCE PREP:

Chop onion and green pepper. Slice celery. Cook macaroni according to package directions. Drain and rinse in cold water. Grate cheese.

PREPARATION:

In large skillet, sauté onion, green pepper and celery in hot oil until softened. Stir in taco seasoning, black beans, kidney beans, tomato sauce and diced tomatoes. Simmer for 10 minutes. Remove from heat. Stir in cooked noodles. Spread bean and noodle mixture into 9x13-inch casserole dish. Wrap with foil; label and freeze. Place grated cheese in small freezer bag; attach to casserole dish.

TO SERVE:

Thaw. Sprinkle grated cheese over top of casserole. Bake uncovered in 375 degree oven for 45 minutes or until center is hot and edges are bubbly.

PER SERVING: 386.0 CALORIES; 2.8G FAT; 21.0G PROTEIN; 71.1G CARBOHYDRATES; 4MG CHOLESTEROL.

Minestrone Soup

6 servings

2 teaspoons olive oil
1 cup onion, chopped
3 garlic cloves, minced
1 cup carrot, thinly sliced
10-oz. potatoes, pared and diced
2 cups cabbage, shredded
2 (16-oz.) cans Italian-style stewed tomatoes, cut up and undrained

1 cup elbow macaroni, uncooked
1 tablespoon basil
½ teaspoon salt
¼ teaspoon pepper
2 (16-oz.) cans white beans
1 cup frozen cut green beans
5 cups water (for serving day)
Parmesan cheese (for serving day)

ADVANCE PREP:

Chop onions. Mince garlic. Slice carrot. Pare and dice potatoes. Shred cabbage.

PREPARATION:

In large saucepan or Dutch oven, sauté onion, garlic and carrots in olive oil over medium-high heat until softened. Add potatoes, cabbage and tomatoes; bring to boil. Remove from heat. Add macaroni, basil, salt, pepper, white beans and green beans. Stir to combine. Don't add water at this time. Cool. Put into labeled freezer bag; seal and freeze.

TO SERVE:

Thaw. Place soup mixture and 5 cups water into Dutch oven or stock pot. Heat until boiling. Sprinkle with Parmesan cheese. Serve.

PER SERVING: 390.3 CALORIES; 3.7G FAT; 21.9G PROTEIN; 71.1G CARBOHYDRATES;3MG CHOLESTEROL.

Vegetarian

Mini-Session #1

Spinach Pizza
Mixed Vegetable Soup
Cajun Stuffed Peppers
Cool Lime Burritos

Shopping List

DAIRY
1 egg
1 (15-oz.) carton reduced-fat ricotta cheese (or cottage cheese)
8-oz. reduced-fat mozzarella cheese
Parmesan cheese
8-oz. reduced-fat grated cheddar cheese

BREAD / PASTA
8 flour tortillas

VEGETABLES
2 large onions
1 bunch green onions
3 garlic cloves
3 large celery stalks
3 large carrots
1 bunch fresh parsley
6 small green, red or yellow bell peppers
1 lime
1 medium cucumber

CANNED / BOXED
1 (8-oz.) jar pizza sauce
2 (16-oz.) cans Italian-style stewed tomatoes, cut up and drained

6 packets instant veggie soup seasoning mix
1 package Cajun-style rice and beans mix
1 (4-oz.) can green chilies
1 (15-oz.) can red kidney beans
1 (15-oz.) can Mexican-style stewed tomatoes

SPICES
2 bay leaves
cumin
cilantro
pepper

FROZEN
1 (16-oz.) loaf frozen bread dough
2 (10-oz.) packages frozen chopped spinach
small package frozen baby lima beans
2 (10-oz.) packages frozen whole kernel corn

MISC.
olive oil
lime juice
white vinegar
honey
Dijon mustard

Preparation Instructions

2 cups onion—chop.

½ cup green onion—slice.

1½ cups celery—slice.

1½ cups carrots—slice.

3 garlic cloves—chop.

6 small bell peppers (red, green or yellow)—cut in half lengthwise; remove seeds and membranes.

1 medium cucumber—peel, seed, and drain.

CHEESE PREP:

8-oz. reduced-fat mozzarella cheese—grate.

4-oz. reduced-fat cheddar cheese—grate.

MISC. PREP:

Frozen bread dough—let frozen dough rise according to package directions; punch down. Cover; let rest 5 minutes before using for pizza.

2 (10-oz.) packages frozen spinach—cook according to package directions; drain well and pat dry.

Spinach Pizza

6 servings

1 (16-oz.) loaf frozen bread
dough, thawed
2 (10-oz.) packages frozen
chopped spinach
½ cup chopped onion
1 garlic clove, minced
1 tablespoon olive oil
1 beaten egg

1 (15-oz.) carton reduced-fat
ricotta cheese
½ cup grated Parmesan cheese
1 (8-oz.) jar pizza sauce
8-oz. (2 cups) grated reduced-
fat mozzarella cheese (for
serving day)

ADVANCE PREP:

Let frozen bread dough rise according to package directions; punch down.
Cover; let rest 5 minutes before using for pizza. Chop onion. Grate mozzarella
cheese. Cook spinach according to package directions; drain well and pat dry.

PREPARATION:

Line 9x13-inch casserole dish with heavy foil. Spray foil lining thoroughly with
cooking spray. Using rolling pin, roll dough into approximately a 14x10-inch
rectangle. Place into foil-lined baking dish, patting onto bottom and up sides.
Prick bottom and sides of dough with fork. Bake dough crust in a 425 degree
oven for 10 minutes or until dough starts to brown. Remove from oven; cool. In
a small skillet, sauté onion and garlic in olive oil until softened; remove from
heat. In medium bowl, combine egg, ricotta, Parmesan, spinach and onion
mixture. Spread over pizza crust. Pour pizza sauce over all. Freeze for 2 hours or
until firm. Lift pizza with foil out of pan. Seal with foil; label and freeze. Place
grated mozzarella in small freezer bag; label, seal and attach to pizza.

TO SERVE:

Do not thaw. Place frozen pizza on baking sheet. Remove top foil. Bake in a
375 degree oven for 1 hour or until heated through. Top with cheese. Bake
about 10 minutes more or till cheese melts. Let stand 5 minutes; remove foil.

*Note: Can be thawed first. Bake in a 375 degree oven for 20 minutes. Top with
cheese. Bake 10 minutes more. Let stand 5 minutes.*

PER SERVING: 514.5 CALORIES; 23.3G FAT; 32.7G PROTEIN; 46.3G CARBOHYDRATES; 73MG CHOLESTEROL.

Mixed Veggie Soup

6 servings

1 cup water
1½ cups onion, diced
1½ cups celery, sliced
1½ cups carrot, sliced
2 (16-oz.) can Italian-style stewed tomatoes, cut up and undrained
1 cup frozen baby lima beans

2 cups frozen whole kernel corn
6 packets instant veggie soup seasoning mix
2 bay leaves
3 tablespoon chopped fresh parsley
½ teaspoon pepper
8 cups water (for serving day)

ADVANCE PREP:

Chop onions. Slice celery and carrots.

PREPARATION:

In large saucepan or Dutch oven, sauté onion, celery, carrots in 1 cup water until softened. Stir in tomatoes, lima beans, corn, seasoning mix, bay leaves, parsley and pepper. Don't add extra water at this time. Place into labeled freezer bags; seal and freeze.

TO SERVE:

Thaw. Put soup and 8 cups water into stockpot. Cook over medium-high heat until heated through.

PER SERVING: 343.5 CALORIES; 5,7G FAT; 13.1G PROTEIN; 64.6G CARBOHYDRATES; 3MG CHOLESTEROL.

Cajun Stuffed Peppers

6 servings

1 (15-oz.) can Mexican-style diced tomatoes, undrained

1½ cups water

1 package Cajun-style rice and beans mix

6 small green, red or yellow bell peppers (or combination)

1 cup (4-oz.) reduced-fat cheddar cheese, grated

ADVANCE PREP:

In saucepan, combine tomatoes, water and rice and beans mix; bring to a boil. Reduce heat and simmer uncovered for ten minutes, or until rice is tender. Cut peppers in half lengthwise; remove seeds and membranes.

PREPARATION:

Place each pepper half in bottom of 9x13-inch casserole dish. Divide rice and beans mixture between pepper halves (approximately ⅓ cup per pepper half). Cover with foil; label and freeze. Place grated cheese into small freezer bag; attach to pan of stuffed peppers.

TO SERVE:

Thaw. Bake, covered, in 350 degree oven for 30 – 40 minutes or until peppers are tender. Uncover; sprinkle with grated cheese. Bake an additional 2 - 3 minutes or until cheese is melted.

PER SERVING: 356.4 CALORIES; 2.3G FAT; 24.2G PROTEIN; 61.7G CARBOHYDRATES; 4MG CHOLESTEROL.

Cool Lime Burritos

8 servings

1 teaspoon grated lime peel
⅓ cup lime juice
2 tablespoon white vinegar
1 tablespoon honey
2 teaspoons Dijon mustard
1 teaspoon cumin
2 garlic cloves, minced
2 tablespoons canned green chilies

1 (10-oz.) package frozen corn kernels
1 (15-oz.) can red kidney beans, drained and rinsed
½ cup sliced green onions
1 medium cucumber, peeled, seeded and diced
2 tablespoons minced cilantro
8 flour tortillas (for serving day)

ADVANCE PREP:

Drain and rinse kidney beans.

PREPARATION:

In a glass bowl, combine lime peel, lime juice, vinegar, honey, mustard, cumin, garlic and chilies. Pour into large freezer bag. Add corn, beans, onions, cucumber and cilantro. Seal bag; rotate to mix vegetables. Place vegetable mixture bag and tortilla bag into a larger bag. Label and freeze.

TO SERVE:

Thaw. Stir to recombine. Drain marinade off vegetable mixture. Discard marinade. Warm tortillas slightly (the filling won't be warmed). Divide mixture between tortillas. Roll to enclose filling.

PER SERVING: 250.9 CALORIES; 3.3G FAT; 10.3G PROTEIN; 47.7G CARBOHYDRATES; 0MG CHOLESTEROL.

Vegetarian
Mini-Session #2

Vegetable Fried Rice
Ricotta Broccoli Pie
Cheese and Veggie Quesadillas
Three Cheese Lasagna

Shopping List

DAIRY
4 cups skim milk
7 eggs
2-oz. gruyere cheese
2-oz. reduced-fat mozzarella cheese
4-oz. reduced-fat Monterey Jack
    cheese
1 cup reduced-fat ricotta cheese
small container fat-free sour cream
Parmesan cheese
margarine

BREAD / PASTA
1 pound green spinach lasagna
    noodles
12 flour tortillas
long grain rice

VEGETABLES
1 large red bell pepper
1 bunch green onions
1 large leek
1 pound carrots
1 orange (for zest)
9 garlic cloves
1 small bunch fresh cilantro

1 fresh ginger root

CANNED / BOXED
6-oz. can black beans
4-oz. can green chilies
1 cup salsa

SPICES
basil
nutmeg
salt
pepper
sugar
flour

FROZEN
2 (10-oz.) packages frozen broccoli
    pieces

MISC.
lime juice
cider vinegar
olive oil
soy sauce
oriental sesame oil
½ cup unsalted peanuts

Preparation Instructions

1 bunch green onions—slice.

1 bunch fresh cilantro—mince.

1½ cups leeks—wash and cut into strips.

1½ cups carrots—slice.

1½ cups red bell pepper—dice.

3 tablespoons fresh ginger root—grate.

9 garlic cloves—mince.

½ cup unsalted peanuts—chop coarsely.

½ teaspoon orange zest—finely grate orange part of orange peel.

CHEESE PREP:

4-oz. reduced-fat Monterey Jack cheese—grate.

2-oz. gruyere cheese—grate.

2-oz. mozzarella cheese—grate.

MISC. PREP:

10-oz. long grain rice—prepare according to package directions.

2 (10-oz.) packages frozen broccoli—thaw, drain and chop.

1 pound green spinach lasagna noodles—prepare according to package directions; rinse gently in cold water.

Vegetable Fried Rice

6 servings

1½ cups long grain rice
4 eggs, beaten
½ cup green onions, sliced
½ cup fresh cilantro, minced
2 tablespoons soy sauce
½ teaspoon sugar
1 tablespoon oriental sesame oil
1½ cups washed leeks, cut into thin strips

1½ cups carrot, thinly sliced
1½ cups red bell pepper, diced
3 tablespoons fresh ginger root, grated
6 garlic cloves, minced
½ cup unsalted peanuts, chopped coarsely
3 tablespoons cider vinegar
½ teaspoon salt

ADVANCE PREP:

Cook rice according to package directions. Slice green onion, leeks and carrots. Chop bell pepper. Grate fresh ginger root. Mince garlic. Chop peanuts.

PREPARATION:

In bowl, combine eggs, half of the green onions, sugar, half of the cilantro, half of the soy sauce and 2 tablespoons water. Spray large skillet with cooking spray. Over medium-high heat, scramble egg mixture until no longer wet. In another large skillet, heat oil over medium-high heat; sauté leeks, carrots and bell pepper until softened. Remove from heat. Add ginger and garlic. Stir to combine. Add rice, peanuts, vinegar, salt, egg mixture, remaining green onions, cilantro and soy sauce. Place into large labeled freezer bag; seal and freeze.

TO SERVE:

Thaw. Reheat in large skillet over medium-high heat until heated through. Add a small amount of sesame oil while warming if too dry.

PER SERVING: 333.5 CALORIES; 12.1G FAT; 12.1G PROTEIN; 46.7G CARBOHYDRATES; 144MG CHOLESTEROL.

Ricotta Broccoli Pie

6 servings

1 cup reduced-fat ricotta cheese
1 cup skim milk
3 eggs
¼ cup Parmesan cheese
½ teaspoon orange zest (finely grated orange part of orange peel)

2 teaspoons olive oil
3 garlic cloves, minced
10-oz. package frozen broccoli, thawed, drained and chopped
1 tablespoon basil

ADVANCE PREP:

Zest orange peel. Mince garlic.

PREPARATION:

In blender or food processor, combine ricotta cheese, milk and eggs. Blend until smooth. Add Parmesan and orange zest. Process until combined. In large skillet, sauté garlic in olive oil; add broccoli and basil; cook 2 minutes. In large bowl, combine ricotta mixture and broccoli. Pour into labeled freezer bag; seal and freeze.

TO SERVE:

Thaw. Squish bag gently to recombine. Spray 9-inch pie plate with cooking spray. Pour mixture into pie plate. Bake in 350 degree oven for 40 minutes or until lightly browned and set. Let set 10 minutes before slicing.

PER SERVING: 126.3 CALORIES; 5.3G FAT; 13.4G PROTEIN; 7.3G CARBOHYDRATES; 118MG CHOLESTEROL.

Cheese and Veggie Quesadillas

6 servings

12 flour tortillas
4-oz. (1 cup) reduced-fat
    Monterey Jack cheese, grated
1 cup frozen broccoli pieces (or
    fresh)
6-oz. canned black beans,
    drained and rinsed
1 tablespoon lime juice

¼ cup canned green chilies
¼ cup fresh cilantro
¼ cup green onions, sliced
1 cup salsa (mild or medium
    according to taste)
3 tablespoons fat-free sour
    cream (for serving day)

ADVANCE PREP:

Grate cheese. Drain and rinse canned black beans. Cook broccoli until just
tender.

PREPARATION:

In small bowl, mash beans and lime juice to form a paste. Stir in chilies, cilantro
and green onions. Place into labeled freezer bag. Place cooked broccoli into
small freezer bag. In large labeled freezer bag, put the bag of bean mixture, the
bag of cooked broccoli and the bag of tortillas. Seal and freeze.

TO SERVE:

Thaw. Spray two cookie sheets with cooking spray. Place 6 tortillas in a single
layer onto cookie sheets. Spread bean mixture evenly divided between tortillas.
Spread almost to edge of tortilla. Sprinkle broccoli pieces onto bean mixture.
Top each tortilla with remaining tortillas. On two oven racks, bake in 450
degree oven until tortillas are lightly browned (halfway through baking time,
switch cookie sheets in the oven). Slide quesadillas onto cutting board; cut each
into 6 wedges. Serve with cold salsa.

PER SERVING: 463.0 CALORIES; 9.9G FAT; 26.3G PROTEIN; 66.1G CARBOHYDRATES; 15MG CHOLESTEROL.

Three Cheese Lasagna

6 servings

1 pound green spinach lasagna
  noodles
½ cup margarine
6 tablespoons flour
4 cups skim milk
¼ cup Parmesan cheese

2-oz. (½ cup) gruyere cheese,
  grated
2-oz. (½ cup) reduced-fat
  mozzarella, grated
¼ teaspoon salt
⅛ teaspoon pepper
dash nutmeg

ADVANCE PREP:

Prepare green lasagna noodles according to package directions. Rinse in cold
water.

PREPARATION:

In large saucepan, melt the margarine over low heat. Stir in the flour. Heat for 1
minute. Gradually stir in the milk, stirring constantly until thick. Add the
cheeses, salt, pepper and nutmeg to sauce; stir until cheeses melt. Spray a deep
casserole dish with generous amount of cooking spray. Add alternating layers of
lasagna and sauce. Finish with a layer of sauce. Wrap with foil; label and freeze.

TO SERVE:

Thaw. Uncover and sprinkle with a light dusting of Parmesan cheese. Bake in
350 degree oven for 45 minutes until bubbling and golden brown.

PER SERVING: 625.8 CALORIES; 24.8G FAT; 27.8G PROTEIN; 72.7G CARBOHYDRATES; 95MG CHOLESTEROL.

Vegetarian

Mini-Session #3

Dolmas
Baked Spaghetti
Vegetable Quiche
Spicy Chili Mac

Shopping List

DAIRY
2/3 cup non-fat plain yogurt
6-oz. reduced-fat cheddar cheese
2-oz. reduced-fat Swiss cheese
5 eggs
Parmesan cheese

BREAD / PASTA
long grain rice
1 (2-oz.) dry spaghetti noodles
8-oz. elbow macaroni

VEGETABLES
2½ cups onion
1 large cabbage head
4 large carrots
1 bunch green onions
1 lemon
1 small cucumber

CANNED / BOXED
3 (14-oz.) cans diced tomatoes
1½ cups non-fat evaporated milk
3½ cups vegetable broth

1 (15-oz.) can Mexican-style stewed
   tomatoes
1 (15-oz.) can pinto beans
1 (15-oz.) can kidney beans

SPICES
basil
mint
parsley
Italian seasoning
garlic powder
chili powder
red pepper flakes
salt
pepper
flour

MISC.
olive oil
pine nuts
dry currants
soy sauce

Preparation Instructions

1 bunch green onions—slice.

2 large carrots—chop.

2 large carrots—shred.

3 medium onions—chop.

12 large cabbage leaves—trim away tough stems; put leaves into boiling water briefly (about 30 seconds); remove from water using slotted spoon; drain thoroughly.

CHEESE PREP:

6-oz. reduced-fat cheddar cheese—grate.

2-oz. reduced-fat Swiss cheese—grate.

MISC. PREP:

rice—prepare according to package directions to make 1 cup, or use leftover rice.

12-oz. dry spaghetti noodles—prepare according to package directions; drain and rinse in cold water; store in large pan full of cold water in refrigerator until ready to use.

Dolmas

6 servings

12 large cabbage leaves, washed
1 cup long grain rice, uncooked
8 green onions, chopped
1½ teaspoons basil
1½ teaspoons mint
1½ teaspoons parsley

½ cup pine nuts
½ cup currants
½ teaspoon salt
¼ teaspoon pepper
3 tablespoons olive oil

For Dip: (if desired)
juice of 1 lemon
⅔ cup non-fat plain yogurt

¼ cup cucumber, peeled,
seeded and chopped

ADVANCE PREP:

Trim away any tough stems from the cabbage leaves. Put leaves into boiling water briefly, about 30 seconds. Remove from water using slotted spoon; drain thoroughly. Chop green onions.

PREPARATION:

Lay softened cabbage leaves flat on a clean counter top. In large bowl, combine rice, green onions, basil, mint, parsley, pine nuts, currants, salt, pepper and olive oil. Mix the rice mixture thoroughly. Place 2 tablespoons of the rice filling onto each cabbage leaf, pressing it into a sausage shape. Fold the sides of the leaves over the filling and then roll up, jelly roll fashion, to completely enclose the filling. Place filled cabbage rolls seam-side down in a 9x13-inch baking dish. Pour hot water into baking dish until the water comes about halfway up the rolls. Cover baking dish with foil, pressing gently onto rolls. Bake in 375 degree oven for 30 minutes. Remove from oven; cool; wrap, label and freeze.

TO SERVE:

Thaw. Bake in 375 degree oven for 15 minutes or until heated through. Drain the dolmas from the cooking liquid and arrange on a serving plate with a little of the cucumber sauce spooned over, if desired.

Note: While baking dolmas, prepare cucumber yogurt dip, if desired. Peel the cucumber and cut in half lengthwise; remove seeds. Chop cucumber into very small pieces; combine with lemon juice and yogurt; chill.

PER SERVING: 392.7 CALORIES; 14.6G FAT; 13.3G PROTEIN; 61.5G CARBOHYDRATES; 0MG CHOLESTEROL.

Baked Spaghetti

6 servings

12-oz. spaghetti noodles,
  cooked
3 (14-oz.) cans diced tomatoes
1½ cups onion, chopped
2 teaspoons Italian seasoning

4-oz. (1 cup) reduced-fat
  cheddar cheese, grated
3 tablespoons grated Parmesan
  cheese

ADVANCE PREP:

Cook spaghetti noodles according to package directions until just cooked. Chop onions. Grate cheese.

PREPARATION:

Spray 9x13-inch baking dish with cooking spray. Place spaghetti in bottom of pan. Pour tomatoes over the top. Add onion; sprinkle with Italian seasoning. Sprinkle cheddar cheese over the top of the spaghetti mixture; top with Parmesan cheese. Cover with foil; label and freeze.

TO SERVE:

Thaw. Bake in 350 degree oven for 30 - 35 minutes, or until hot and bubbly.

PER SERVING: 289.6 CALORIES; 3.4G FAT; 14.1G PROTEIN; 50.7G CARBOHYDRATES; 6MG CHOLESTEROL.

Vegetable Quiche

6 servings

Crust:

1 cup rice, cooked (white or
  brown)

1 egg, beaten

1 teaspoon soy sauce

Filling:

2-oz. (½ cup) reduced-fat
  cheddar cheese, grated

2-oz. (½ cup) reduced-fat Swiss
  cheese, grated

½ cup carrot, shredded

¼ cup green onion, sliced

1 tablespoon flour

4 eggs, beaten (or equivalent
  egg substitute)

1½ cups non-fat evaporated
  milk

¼ teaspoon salt

¼ teaspoon pepper

¼ teaspoon garlic powder

ADVANCE PREP:

Cook rice (or use leftover rice for crust). Grate cheeses. Shred carrots. Slice
green onions.

PREPARATION:

Crust: Mix together cooked rice, egg and soy sauce. Spray 9-inch pie plate with
cooking spray. Spread rice mixture evenly to cover pie plate. Bake rice crust at
350 for 10 minutes. Remove from oven.

FILLING:

In mixing bowl, combine together cheeses, carrot, green onion and flour.
Sprinkle over bottom of quiche crust. In bowl, combine eggs, milk, salt, pepper
and garlic powder. Pour over cheese/vegetable mixture. Bake in 375 degree oven
for 45 minutes or until knife inserted near center comes out clean. Remove
from oven. Let stand 10 minutes before slicing if serving right away or freezing
in slices. Cool completely. Wrap with foil; label and freeze.

TO SERVE:

Thaw. Serve cold. Or heat in 350 degree oven for 15 minutes until heated
through.

PER SERVING: 192.1 CALORIES; 5.1G FAT; 15.7G PROTEIN; 19.8G CARBOHYDRATES; 185MG CHOLESTEROL.

Spicy Chili Mac

6 servings

2 large carrots, chopped
1 cup onion, chopped
¼ cup water
3½ cups vegetable broth
1 (15-oz.) can Mexican-style stewed tomatoes, cut up and don't drain
1 (15-oz.) can pinto beans, undrained

1 (15-oz.) can red kidney beans, undrained
3 tablespoons chili powder
8-oz. elbow macaroni, uncooked
½ teaspoon salt
½ teaspoon crushed red pepper flakes

ADVANCE PREP:

Chop carrots and onion.

PREPARATION:

In large skillet, cook carrots and onion in ¼ cup water until somewhat softened. Remove from heat. Add broth, tomatoes, pinto beans and kidney beans (and the liquid from the cans of beans), chili powder, salt and red pepper flakes. Stir in macaroni. Place in large labeled freezer bag; seal and freeze.

TO SERVE:

Thaw. Reheat over medium-high heat until heated through. Serve with non-fat plain yogurt or non-fat sour cream spooned on top, if desired.

PER SERVING: 336.8 CALORIES; 3.9G FAT; 13.5G PROTEIN; 63.2G CARBOHYDRATES; 1MG CHOLESTEROL.

Eggplant Mini-Session

Classic Ratatouille
Eggplant Bake
Stuffed Eggplant
Eggplant Penne

Shopping List

DAIRY
Parmesan cheese
1½ cups nonfat plain yogurt
4-oz. reduced-fat cheddar cheese
margarine

BREAD / PASTA
10-oz. penne pasta
long grain rice

VEGETABLES
4 medium eggplants
3 small eggplants
6 medium zucchini
1 green bell pepper
1 red bell pepper
6 large onions
8 garlic cloves
12 large tomatoes

CANNED / BOXED
2 (16-oz.) cans crushed tomatoes

2 (16-oz.) cans stewed tomatoes
1 (4-oz.) can green chilies

SPICES
rosemary
salt
pepper
sugar
red pepper flakes
basil
parsley
chili powder
turmeric
marjoram
cinnamon

MISC.
olive oil
vegetable oil
red wine vinegar
malt vinegar

Preparation Instructions

4-oz. reduced-fat cheddar cheese—grate.

VEGETABLE PREP:

3 small eggplants—wrap in foil and bake 20 minutes at 350 degrees to soften. Remove from oven; allow to cool. Cut eggplants in half; carefully scoop out pulp leaving a 1-inch thick shell. Reserve scooped out pulp.

2 medium eggplants—cut into 1-inch cubes.

2 medium eggplants—cut into ¼-inch thick slices.

2 large onions—chop.

4 large onions—peel and slice into rings.

7 garlic cloves—mince.

6 medium zucchini—halve lengthwise and slice thickly.

1 green bell pepper—seed and cut into chunks.

1 red bell pepper—seed and cut into chunks.

4 large tomatoes—cut into chunks.

MISC. PREP:

Long grain rice—prepare 1 cup cooked rice.

Classic Ratatouille

8 servings

⅓ cup olive oil
2 large onions, sliced
2 garlic cloves, minced
1 medium eggplant, cut into
    ½-inch cubes
6 medium zucchini, halved
    lengthwise and thickly sliced
1 green pepper, seeded and cut
    into chunks

1 red pepper, seeded and cut
    into chunks
1 teaspoon salt
1 teaspoon basil
½ cup parsley
4 large tomatoes, cut into
    chunks

ADVANCE PREP:

Slice onions. Mince garlic. Cube eggplant. Slice zucchini. Seed and cut green and red peppers into chunks. Cut tomatoes into chunks.

PREPARATION:

In large skillet, sauté onions and garlic over high heat in olive oil until softened. Add eggplant, zucchini, peppers, salt, basil and parsley. Cover pan and cook over medium-low heat for 30 minutes. If mixture becomes dry, add ¼ cup of water. If mixture becomes too soupy and wet, remove cover. Add tomato chunks. Cook for an additional 10 minutes. Remove from heat. Cool. Pour into large labeled freezer bag; seal and freeze.

TO SERVE:

Thaw. Reheat over medium heat until heated through. Can be served hot or cold.

PER SERVING: 148.3 CALORIES; 9.5G FAT; 3.2G PROTEIN; 15.6G CARBOHYDRATES; 0MG CHOLESTEROL.

Eggplant Bake

6 servings

2 medium-sized eggplants, cut into ¼-inch thick slices

2½ teaspoons salt

⅔ cup malt vinegar

2½ tablespoons vegetable oil

2 large onions, peeled and sliced into rings

1 (4-oz.) can green chilies

1 (16-oz.) can stewed tomatoes, cut up and drained

¾ teaspoon chili powder

1 garlic clove, minced

¾ teaspoons ground turmeric

8 tomatoes, sliced

1 ½ cups non-fat plain yogurt

1 ¼ teaspoons ground black pepper

4-oz. (1 cup) reduced-fat cheddar cheese, grated

ADVANCE PREP:

Slice eggplant into ¼-inch thick slices. Slice onions into rings. Slice tomatoes. Grate cheese. Arrange the slices in a shallow baking dish and sprinkle with 1 ½ teaspoons of the salt. Pour the malt vinegar over the top, cover and marinate 30 minutes. Drain eggplant well; discard marinade liquid.

PREPARATION:

In large skillet, heat the vegetable oil and gently sauté onion rings until golden brown. Add chilies, remaining salt, chopped stewed tomatoes, chili powder, garlic and turmeric. Mix well; simmer for 5 minutes. Remove sauce from heat and cool slightly. In blender or food processor, blend to a smooth puree. Arrange half the eggplant slices in base of shallow ovenproof dish sprayed with cooking spray. Spoon half the tomato sauce over eggplant slices; cover with remaining eggplant; top with remaining tomato sauce and sliced tomatoes. In small bowl, combine yogurt, black pepper and cheddar cheese. Pour over tomato slices. Bake in 350 degree oven for 20 minutes. Remove from oven; cool. Wrap with foil; label and freeze.

TO SERVE:

Thaw. Bake in 375 degree oven for 15 minutes or until heated through and topping is golden brown. Serve hot straight from the oven.

PER SERVING: 242.0 CALORIES; 9.5G FAT; 10.9G PROTEIN; 33.7G CARBOHYDRATES; 10MG CHOLESTEROL.

Stuffed Eggplant

6 servings

3 small eggplants
3 tablespoons margarine
1 large onion, finely chopped
2 cloves garlic, minced
1 (16-oz.) can stewed tomatoes,
   drained and cut up

1 cup long grain rice, cooked
3 teaspoons fresh chopped
   marjoram
pinch cinnamon
½ teaspoon salt
¼ teaspoon pepper

ADVANCE PREP:

Preheat oven to 350 degrees. Wrap eggplants in aluminum foil and bake 20 minutes to soften. Remove from oven; allow to cool. Cut the eggplants in half; carefully scoop out pulp leaving 1-inch thick shell. Reserve scooped out pulp. Chop onions. Cook rice.

PREPARATION:

In large skillet, sauté onion and garlic in melted margarine until softened. Chop the eggplant pulp roughly; stir into skillet with onions. Cover and cook for 5 minutes. Stir tomatoes, rice, marjoram, cinnamon, salt and pepper into cooked eggplant. Carefully pile rice into eggplant shells. Wrap each stuffed eggplant half with aluminum foil. Place individually wrapped eggplants into large labeled freezer bag; seal and freeze.

TO SERVE:

Thaw. Take eggplant halves out of freezer bag; keep wrapped in foil. Place onto cookie sheet, bake in 350 degree oven for 20 minutes.

PER SERVING: 241.6 CALORIES; 6.4G FAT; 5.4G PROTEIN; 44.1G CARBOHYDRATES; 0MG CHOLESTEROL.

Eggplant Penne

6 servings

10-oz. penne pasta
2 teaspoons olive oil
1 cup onion, chopped
3 garlic cloves, minced
1 medium eggplant, diced
½ cup water
2 cups canned crushed
  tomatoes

2 teaspoons red wine vinegar
½ teaspoon rosemary
½ teaspoon salt
½ teaspoon sugar
¼ teaspoon red pepper flakes
¼ cup Parmesan cheese (for
  serving
  day)

ADVANCE PREP:

Chop onion. Mince garlic. Dice eggplant.

PREPARATION:

In large skillet, sauté onion and garlic in hot oil until onion is softened. Add eggplant and ½ cup water; boil; reduce heat to low, cover, and simmer 5 minutes. Remove from heat. Stir in tomatoes, vinegar, rosemary, salt, sugar and red pepper flakes. Cool. Place into labeled freezer bag; seal and freeze.

TO SERVE:

Thaw. Cook penne according to package directions. Heat eggplant/tomato mixture in large skillet over medium-high heat until heated through. Toss penne and eggplant mixture together. Sprinkle with Parmesan cheese.

PER SERVING: 254.3 CALORIES; 6.4G FAT; 9.4G PROTEIN; 46.9G CARBOHYDRATES; 3MG CHOLESTEROL.

APPENDIX A

Freezing Times Chart

Freezing for longer than the recommended times could mean a less than perfect food item after thawing. For best results, use the following guidelines.

Baked goods (breads, muffins, rolls) = 2 to 3 months

Beef (ground), cooked = 2 to 3 months

Beef (ground), raw = 4 to 6 months

Beef (non-ground), cooked = 4 to 6 months

Beef (non-ground), raw = 7 to 9 months

Casseroles = 2 to 6 months

Chili = 4 to 6 months

Cookies = 4 to 6 months

Fish, cooked = 2 to 3 months

Fish, raw pieces = 12 months

Gravy = 1 to 2 months

Meatloaf, meatballs = 3 to 4 months

Meat pies = 2 months

Pancakes / Waffles, cooked = 6 months

Pasta recipes = 2 to 3 months

Pizza = 2 months

Pizza dough = 6 months

Pork, cooked = 1 to 2 months

Potatoes, cooked = 1 to 2 months

Poultry, cooked = 2 to 3 months

Poultry, raw = 9 - 12 months

Quiche (cooked or uncooked) = 3 months

Rice, cooked = 3 to 4 months

Sauces = 4 to 6 months

Seafood, cooked = 2 months

Seafood, raw = 12 months

Soups, stews = 2 to 3 months

Vegetables, blanched = 10 to 12 months

Recipe Equivalents

Recipes will often call for two cups of diced onions or three cups of grated cheese. This can make it difficult to decipher how many whole onions to buy or how many pounds of cheese to add to your shopping list. The following list of equivalents is approximate.

Vegetables / Fruits

1 medium onion = 1 cup diced
1 medium green pepper = 1 cup diced
3 ounces fresh mushrooms = 1 cup sliced
1 pound carrots = 3 cups sliced or diced
2 large celery ribs = 1 cup sliced or diced
1 medium tomato = 1 cup chopped
1 medium clove garlic = 1 teaspoon minced
1 medium potato = 1 cup sliced or chopped
1 medium apple = 1 cup chopped
1 lemon = 3 tablespoons juice
1 orange = • cup juice

Dairy

4 ounces (¼ pound) cheese = 1 cup grated or cubed
1 pound block of cheese = 4 cups grated
   or cubed
1 cup heavy whipping cream = 2 cups
   whipped
2 cups margarine or butter = 1 pound

Bread / Pasta / Rice / Beans

1½ slices bread = 1 cup soft crumbs
24 saltine crackers = 1 cup fine crumbs
8 ounces dry noodles = 4 - 5 cups cooked
12 ounces dry spaghetti = 4 cups cooked
1 cup uncooked rice = 3 cups cooked
1 cup dry white beans = 2½ cups cooked

Meats

1 pound ground beef or turkey = 2½ cups
   browned
3 - 4 pound whole chicken = 4 cups
   cooked meat
1 medium chicken breast = 1 cup cubed
1 pound ham = 3 cups cubed or ground
8 slices bacon = ½ cup crumbled
1 pound stew meat = 2 cups cubed

Misc.

¼ pound nuts = 1 cup chopped

Recommended

Resources

Freezer Meal Books

I've discovered that many people who enjoy cooking for the freezer also like to collect cookbooks on the topic. If you're looking for more information, there's a great deal available. If you order one of these books directly from the author, be sure to mention that you read about their resources in *Frozen Assets Lite and Easy*. As an author, I know it's always helpful and fun to discover how people first find out about your books.

Several of the listed resources are currently out-of-print. If you're interested in reading these books, check with your local library to see if they're available through an inter-library loan. I found copies of these out-of-print resources at local yard sales and thrift stores.

NOTE: My two *Frozen Assets* books and the book, *Once-a-Month Cooking*, are the only freezer cooking books I've found that provide prepared meal plans. The other books require the reader to develop their own meal plans from the included recipes.

Frozen Assets: how to cook for a day and eat for a month, by Deborah Taylor-Hough. Champion Press, Ltd. My original freezer-meal book. Inexpensive recipes, step-by-step instructions, money-saving ideas, family-friendly. Contains a complete 30 Day Meal Plan, Two Week Meal Plan and special Ten-Day Holiday Meal Plan. Available through bookstores and libraries.

Bake and Freeze Chocolate Desserts, by Elinor Klivans. Broadway Books. Wow! Chocolate cooking for the freezer! 120 recipes for chocolate treats that can be made ahead frozen to be eaten weeks, even months, later. Great idea during the holidays. Available through bookstores and libraries.

Cooking Ahead, by Mary Carney. Simple Living Workshops. As a home schooling mother of four, minister's wife, frequent seminar speaker, and free-lance writer, Mary Carney has depended on her Cooking Ahead techniques to simplify her busy life. For ordering information, write to: Mary Carney, c/o Simple Living Workshops, P.O. Box 174, Advance, Indiana 46102.

Cooking for the Freezer, by Myra Waldo.
An older book. Excellent for examples of the types of things that freeze well. Out-of-print.

Cook Now, Serve Later, by Readers' Digest Books.
A full-range general cookbook of 425 recipes especially designed to be prepared in advance and stored in the refrigerator or freezer. Available in bookstores and libraries.

Dinner's in the Freezer: More Mary and Less Martha, by Jill Bond. Holly Hall Publishing. Contains general information on Christian homemaking, including some information on cooking for the freezer. Helpful charts. Available through bookstores and libraries.

Do-Ahead Cookbook, by Ann H. Harvey. Oxmoor House. Large format, hard-bound book. A large number of recipes for the freezer along with recipes that aren't frozen, but can be prepared hours (or days!) ahead of time to be served later. Available through bookstores and libraries.

Don't Panic ... It's in the Freezer!, by Susie Martinez, Bonnie Garcia and Vanda Howell. This book was developed by a group of friends that cooked together and then began sharing what they were doing with others. Small, spiral-bound, lays flat, nice collection of recipes. Order from the author by sending $13.95 + $3 shipping and handling payable to: Don't Panic ... It's in the Freezer!, P.O. Box 150851, Lakewood, Colorado 80226.

Farm Journal Freezing and Canning Cookbook, from Food Editors at Farm Journal. Farm Journal. Country women have always been known for their well-stocked pantries. Tips, recipes, helpful hints. Out-of-print.

Fix & Freeze Cookbook, by Better Homes and Gardens. Excellent recipes, tips, full-color photographs. Out-of-print.

The Freezer Cooking Manual, by Nanci Slagle and Tara Wohlenhaus. 30 Day Gourmet. This is the updated version of the 30 Day Gourmet notebook. Emphasizes sharing your cooking day with a friend. Charts and planning sheets to simplify cooking with someone else. Photos, humor, spiral-bound. Order from the authors by sending $14.95 + $3 shipping and handling payable to: 30 Day Gourmet, P.O. Box 272, Brownsburg, Indiana 46112.

Guests Without Stress Cookbook, by Elizabeth Hill. Howell Press. Recipes and menus to make ahead. Available in bookstores and libraries.

Make-Ahead Cook Book, by Better Homes and Gardens. Recipes to make now and serve later. Not necessarily always designed for freezer cooking. Out-of-print.

Month of Meals, by Kelly Machel. Krm de la Krm Publishing. Small, three-ring binder format. Friendly recipes. Order from the author by sending $21.95 + $3 shipping and handling (WA residents add 8.6% sales tax) payable to: KRM de la KRM Publishing, 323 Williams Ave. S., Renton, Washington 98055.

Once-a-Month Cooking, by Mimi Wilson and Mary Beth Lagerborg. Broadman & Holman Publishers. This book revolutionized the way I feed my family. The recipes are a bit on the gourmet/expensive side. Several complete meal plans including a low-fat two-week version. Available through bookstores and libraries.

Once and For All Cooking, by Stephanie Stephens. The Family Cookery. Spiral-bound, large format. The author is a gourmet-trained cook and the recipes are geared toward gourmet tastes (may not be appealing to small children, but the recipes look tasty to me). Order from the author by sending $19.95 + $3 shipping and handling to: The Family Cookery, P.O. Box 1017, San Leandro, California 94577.

Prevention's Low-Fat, Low-Cost Freezer Cookbook, by Sharon Sanders. Rodale Press. Quick dishes for—and from—the freezer. Over 220 recipes. Published by Prevention Health Books. Available through bookstores and libraries.

Cooking-Related Books

365 Quick, Easy and Inexpensive Dinner Menus, by Penny E. Stone. Champion Press, Ltd. This book contains more simple to prepare, family-pleasing recipes than I've ever seen collected into a single volume. Available in bookstores and libraries.

Cheapskate in the Kitchen, by Mary Hunt. St Martin's. Learn to prepare delicious gourmet meals for a fraction of the cost of restaurant dining. I contributed several recipes to this book. Available in bookstores and libraries.

Desperation Dinners, by Beverly Mills and Alicia Ross. Workman Publishing. The answer to every desperate cook's prayers. Features delicious, healthy, home-cooked meals that can be prepared in 20 minutes. Available in bookstores and libraries.

Eat Healthy for $50 a Week, by Rhonda Barfield. Kensington Publishing Corporation. Feed your family nutritious delicious meals for less. Yes, it really is possible to feed your family healthy meals for $50 per week. Barfield shows you how (recipes included). Available in bookstores and libraries.

Healthy Foods: an irreverent guide to understanding nutrition and feeding your family well, by Leanne Ely C.N.C. Champion Press, Ltd. *www.championpress.com.* This fun and practical cookbook will take you step-by-step through nutrition fundamentals and provide over 100 taste-tested recipes that even the kids will love. Being healthy has never been easier!

Mix-n-Match Recipes, by Deborah Taylor-Hough. Champion Press, Ltd. *www.championpress.com* Simple and creative recipes using common ingredients. A great way to use up leftovers. Soup, quiche, skillet meals, casseroles, dessert breads, and more. Available in bookstores and libraries.

More-With-Less Cookbook, by Doris Longacre. Herald Press. The classic, thoughtful cookbook published by the Mennonites. Every kitchen needs this book on the shelf. Available in bookstores and libraries.

The New Laurel's Kitchen, by Laurel Robertson. Ten Speed Press. Whole foods cooking at it's best. Available in bookstores and libraries.

Not Just Beans, by Tawra Jean Kellam. Not Just Beans. Fifty years of frugal family favorites. Over 500 recipes and 400+ tips. Comb-binding. To order from the author, send $14.95 + $3.50 shipping and handling payable to: Not Just Beans, P.O. Box 131, Manhattan, Kansas 66505

Make-A-Mix, by Karine Eliason. Fisher Books. Make your own healthy homemade mixes. Save time and money, plus you control the ingredients so you know the mixes are healthy for your family. Many mixes make great gift ideas, too. Available in bookstores and libraries.

On-Line Resources

Frozen Assets Web Pages
   http://hometown.aol.com/OAMCLoop/index.html
   Dedicated to freezer meal cooking techniques. Recipes, tips, Message Board, many helpful freezer-related links.

A Frugal, Simple Life
   http://hometown.aol.com/DSimple/index.html
   Tips, quotes, articles, Message Board, lots of links.

Frugal Books for Simple Living

http://hometown.aol.com/DSimple/books.html

Small on-line bookstore of frugal and simple living books. Many of the books listed in this Appendix can be ordered on-line from this web-page. (Operated in association with Amazon.com.)

Busy Cooks

http://busycooks.about.com/

Regular features on freezer meals, planned leftovers, quick cooking recipes, easy entertaining, more.

http://www.rushhourcook.com

Foolproof recipes and menus for busy families.

OTHER GREAT COOKBOOKS BY CHAMPION PRESS, LTD. AUTHORS:

Frozen Assets: how to cook for a day and eat for a month by Deborah Taylor-Hough

Mix and Match Recipes by Deborah Taylor-Hough

Crazy About Crockpots: 101 Easy and Inexpensive Recipes for .75 cents or less a servings by Penny E. Stone

Crazy About Crockpots: 101 Easy and Inexpensive Recipes to Entertain at less than .75 cents or less a servings by Penny E. Stone

Crazy About Crockpots: 101 Soup and Stew Recipes for .75 cents or less a servings by Penny E. Stone

365 Quick, Easy and Inexpensive Dinner Menus by Penny E. Stone

Healthy Foods: an irreverent guide to understanding nutrition and feeding your family well by Leanne Ely, C.N.C.

Healthy Foods: A Practical Guide to Nutrition and Wellness (for Grades K-5 or for Grades 6-9) by Leanne Ely, C.N.C.

The Frantic Family Cookbook: Mostly Healthy Meals in Minutes by Leanne Ely, C.N.C.

Cooking for Blondes by Rhonda Levitch

The Rush Hour Cook: Weekly Wonders by Brook Noel

The Rush Hour Cook: Effortless Entertaining by Brook Noel

The Rush Hour Cook: One-Pot Wonders by Brook Noel

The Rush Hour Cook: Family Favorites by Brook Noel

The Rush Hour Cook: Pasta Presto by Brook Noel

For more information on all of the great titles

Champion Press, Ltd. has to offer visit www.championpress.com

CHAMPION PRESS LTD.

Use coupon code 633 to take $5 off your first order